The
PROFESSIONAL COACH

Cultivate CREDIBILITY,
Attract HIGH-PAYING CLIENTS,
and Create A THRIVING BUSINESS

MELINDA COHAN

MIRASEE PRESS

5750 Avenue Notre Dame de Grace
Montreal, Quebec
H4A 1M4, Canada
www.mirasee.com

Copyright © 2024 by Melinda Cohan

All rights reserved. This book, or parts thereof, may not be reproduced in any form without permission.

Paperback ISBN: 979-8-9891641-4-1
Hardback ISBN: 979-8-9891641-5-8
E-book ISBN: 979-8-9891641-6-5

1 3 5 7 9 10 8 6 4 2

Praise for
THE PROFESSIONAL COACH

Wise. Authentic. Clear and straight to the point. And what sets this book apart is its focus on 'Sustainability in Business,' where Melinda addresses the crucial aspect of maintaining high-performance levels without burning out. She provides a Comprehensive Going Pro Checklist with actionable steps that ensure continuous improvement and sustained success. Any coach with a big dream will benefit from this transformational manuscript.

SAGE LAVINE, WomenRockingBusiness.com

Everything Melinda Cohan creates delivers practical steps to rock your coaching business. And this book is her best yet! It tackles all the topics (inner and outer game) that stop coaches from achieving their dream business. The format of the book makes it easy to read and I loved the surprise 'gift' at the end of each chapter. If you want to be a profitable coach without selling your soul, 'The Professional Coach' will quickly become your coaching business bible!

JEANNA GABELLINI, business coach
and author of Rock Your Profits

This book is an indispensable guide for elevating your practice to new heights. It really drives home the critical importance of professionalizing your coaching business and provides clear strategies for building sustainable success. The practical steps for setting competitive prices, optimizing business operations, and blending spiritual wisdom with professional advice, are invaluable as you work to build a thriving, soul-aligned business.

DANNY INY, best-selling author of
Teach Your Gift and Effortless

If you're looking to streamline your coaching business, 'The Professional Coach' by Melinda Cohan is a must-read. The chapter on 'Implementing Business Operations' is a gem, packed with practical tips to help you run things more efficiently. Melinda shows you how to optimize workflows and handle admin tasks so you can focus more on coaching. This chapter is a game-changer. I definitely recommend it for any coach wanting to boost productivity!

MARGARET LYNCH RANIERE, empowerment coach and
best-selling author of *Unblocked*

Melinda is a leading expert in coaching business success, and she offers straightforward advice to help you streamline your processes, set the right prices, and keep your clients happy. Whether you're just starting out or ready to grow, this book gives you the tools to build a successful and sustainable coaching business — without the stress.

ABE CRYSTAL, founder of Ruzuku and
author of *The Business of Courses*

A must-have resource for elevating your coaching practice. If you are struggling with structuring, pricing, and streamlining your business, 'The Professional Coach' by Melinda Cohan is your go-to guide for practical, actionable steps toward growth. The chapter on 'Setting Professional Pricing' alone will shift your perspective on charging your worth and confidently standing in how you price your services. Stop whatever you are doing and get this book. It will quickly become your coaching practice favorite.

JANE DEUBER, founder of Magpai,
the world's leading gap-assessment software

If you're a coach ready to build a profitable practice while staying true to your values, grab yourself a copy of Melinda Cohan's 'The Professional Coach.' In this deeply valuable resource, Melinda will guide you through the practicalities of business, helping you shine brightly in the coaching industry. Melinda's approach is a perfect blend of practical wisdom and inspirational guidance.

BARBARA HUSON, author of *Overcoming Undearearning*
and *Secrets of Six-Figure Women*

'The Professional Coach' is a must-read for aspiring and established coaches alike. Melinda Cohan combines moving stories, hard-won wisdom, and a brilliantly honed success road map to guide readers through the intricacies of building a thriving coaching practice. This book is profound, fascinating, and utterly practical. If you're a coach or want to be, and you want to make a good living, this is the book for you.

OCEAN ROBBINS, Cofounder & CEO,
Food Revolution Network

Melinda has an exceptional talent for demystifying complex ideas, and her simple, highly actionable steps provide a clear path to professional success. This book is more than just a read; it's an adventure that equips you to make the most of your coaching career!

TRACY GARRIGAN, CHHC,
Founding Director & Program Manager of
Food Revolution Network's Plant-Based
Coaching Certification

Every dream or vision sounds good in theory. But actually doing and being what it takes to live that dream, is another thing entirely. In 'The Professional Coach' Melinda Cohan blends her vast experience as a highly successful coach and mentor to thousands of coaches with her innate ability to get to the heart of things in a deep and profound way that just makes sense! This book is a "How To" manual for all coaches who are courageously crossing over from the idea of being a coach to actually living a fulfilling life as a highly paid, highly successful coach with a thriving business making a difference in the world.

MICHELLE FALZON, marketing & content strategist
for world-renowned coaches

If you're looking to grow your coaching business, 'The Professional Coach' is your ultimate guide. Melinda takes you on an empowering journey from the initial stages of dabbling in coaching to running a full-fledged, thriving business. Her candid storytelling, coupled with actionable strategies, makes this book a treasure trove for new and seasoned coaches alike. This is not just a book; it's a step-by-step blueprint for success. Dive in and watch your coaching dreams become a reality!

DAVID NEWMAN, author of *Do It! Marketing* and *Do It! Selling*

'The Professional Coach' is a game-changer. Melinda breaks down complex concepts into easy-to-understand steps in key areas like setting professional pricing, creating your unique value proposition, and more. Her practical advice, combined with strategic insights, makes this book a must-read for coaches at any stage of their career who want to thrive in today's competitive marketplace.

MICHELLE SCHUBNEL, Group Coaching Expert

Melinda provides the most comprehensive yet easy-to-follow pathway for making your mark as a powerful, profitable, and productive coach. Put simply, if you really want to create the business and lifestyle you deserve while fully serving your clients and the world, then the message is clear: It's time to up your game and this book provides the perfect 'what and how guide' for making it happen.

PETER SAGE, multiple best-selling author, coach, speaker and chief visionary officer for the Sage Academy

To all the courageous coaches who say YES! to their dreams and start their own business.

To the women and Sisters in my life that have inspired and helped shape me to be the woman I am today.

And to my husband for being my CPO and supporting my dreams.

Download the Audiobook + The Professional Coaching Business Tool Kit (for FREE)!

READ THIS FIRST

Just to say thank you for reading my book, I'd love to share the audiobook version PLUS the accompanying Professional Coaching Business Tool Kit, at no cost whatsoever. It's my gift to you.

—Melinda Cohan

Go to **https://theprofessionalcoachbook.com/toolkit** to get it!

CONTENTS

FOREWORD	1
INTRODUCTION	7
NAVIGATING THE BOOK: Making the Most of Your Business Adventure	17
The Natural Evolution of a Coaching Business	27
The Path to Professionalism	39
PILLAR 1: Expanding Commitment and Dedication	55
PILLAR 2: Defining Work Ethic	75
PILLAR 3: Creating Your Unique Value Proposition	93
PILLAR 4: Establishing Accountability for Outcomes	111
PILLAR 5: Designing Delivery of Client Support	133
PILLAR 6: Setting Professional Pricing	155
PILLAR 7: Managing Business Finances	177
PILLAR 8: Implementing Business Operations	205
SUSTAINABILITY IN BUSINESS: Performing at High Levels Without Burning Out	223
CONCLUSION: Practice Makes Progress	249
THE COMPREHENSIVE GOING PRO CHECKLIST	253
ADDITIONAL RESOURCES	259
A REQUEST	261
GRATITUDES	263
REFERENCES	267
ABOUT THE AUTHOR	277

FOREWORD

There I was, attending my first networking meeting, about to introduce myself as a "success coach" since those were the words I had printed on a business card the day before. It was day one of my journey into the business of being a coach (after the less scary part of training to be a coach) and I was pit-sweaty, terrified, and quite sure that I was indeed a fraud.

Fast-forward about six months and I had improved my ability to market myself and had a full roster of clients who wanted to be more successful. I was throwing myself into my work—a chemical engineer turned empowerment coach—and actually delivering results getting them unstuck, motivated, and into action. My heart was singing because I was *really* helping people and it was rewarding and meaningful in a way that my corporate career had not been. *But*, and this is a very big *but*, my bank account was crying because I was *clueless* on the business and money part!

Since I was used to a cushy salary, I had no idea how the business of being a coach worked so I was flailing and failing at things like setting prices, selling more than one session, and having a consistent flow of clients without beating the pavement. I was all over the place, doing good session work while reinventing the marketing wheel and slowly, painfully running out of money. It took me years of trial and error to figure it all out and finally replace my corporate salary doing the work that I loved.

This is why ten years later, I had singled out Melinda Cohan in a room full of very cool people as *the* one I wanted to meet. I was fascinated by what I had heard about her expertise—the streamlining of the business side of coaching, that she somehow—impossibly—had made easy.

I had to meet this wizard with the magic wand that could transform the very things that coaches found the most arduous, painful, and confusing into something effective and efficient. But I wasn't just a curious admirer of her success, because at that point I was well into training and certifying coaches in my breakthrough empowerment coaching framework. The thousands of coaches I was training—they all needed this!

In Melinda, I found a twin soul that had also moved from success in the corporate world to being a coach, and then ventured beyond that into helping others in our beloved field truly succeed. Her driving purpose is to remove the barriers and distractions of business so that coaches can *thrive* helping others while the business part practically runs on autopilot. I have never met anyone more passionate about automated systems, software, and workflows, who could then turn on a dime and blow away a room with the power of heart, then launch into Dance-Party mode to shift energy! Yes, one cool lady!

FOREWORD

I am thrilled she has decided to distill her genius into this fabulous book. It includes a healthy dose of clarity from the start—do you *really* want to be a coach? And if so, do you really want to make this your next chapter career as a professional coach?

Assuming your answer is "I am all in!" Cohan lays out the eight pillars of professionalism needed to move from a coach with some skills into being and earning as a thriving professional.

As I read her eight pillars, I realize that I would have named this book *Everything I Wish I Knew When I Started Coaching*. I became a coach to follow my heart and do something that made me feel alive and fulfilled, but as a single mother, I could not be an amateur. I needed to learn the real business skills to be a success as a coach both in what I was giving AND receiving ... and that took me way too long! As a matter of fact, I almost gave up my dream and went back to corporate America several times.

Melinda knows this story so well—my story and the story of thousands of coaches we have met over the years—of being so passionate about helping others as a new coach and then coming to a screeching halt when things get *real*. It is frustrating and truly heartbreaking when our dream becomes a disappointment, and our calling is something we start to doubt because we didn't know how to break free of the amateur level or understand what it means to have a business. I have watched Melinda work tirelessly to show coaches the better, faster, leveraged way to turn their passion into a real business...a professional business.

Part of her gift is the way her brain works and the other part of it is her spirit. You will notice throughout the book Melinda has carefully chosen oracle cards to bring your heart and your spirit into this process. I know you will find these moments of reflection and integration powerful, centering, and provocative as you work through the eight pillars. This is true to her essence as an advocate for life balance, joy, and deliciousness in harmony with serious, kick-ass professionalism.

So now it is your time to choose. Be honest with yourself about what you really want from coaching—not just what you want to give, but what you want to receive and who you want to BE as a coach. A hobbyist? An amateur? Or . . . a professional? My favorite part of the book is this exact, overarching theme of honesty—get clear and be honest with yourself—that Melinda holds the reader to in her lovingly fierce way.

The call to clarity and commitment, together with the strategies that have been honed and sharpened over many years, has allowed her to help thousands of real people become truly thriving, empowered, happy coaches.

For those of you who answer the call, *The Professional Coach* will lay out the path for you, step-by-step, for rapid growth, earning what you truly deserve, and creating a lifestyle business that you will love. This book will take you from being excited and ready to take your next step . . . to being actually prepared to succeed. From the bottom of my heart, I encourage you because I know that coaches can transform the world, and yes, you CAN do it. Melinda is ready to light

FOREWORD

the way for you with her wisdom, strategies, and spirit of pure positivity.

—Margaret Lynch Raniere
Author of *Unblocked* and *Tapping Into Wealth*,
Coach Trainer, and Speaker

Introduction
SETTING THE STAGE FOR COACHING BUSINESS SUCCESS

I never wanted to be an entrepreneur.

I know, that sounds odd coming from a woman who's owned her own business since 2002.

When I was thirteen years old, I knew I wanted to be an interior designer. While I was getting my Interior Design degree, one of my college professors asked who in my class wanted to get a job in the design field and who wanted to start their own design firm. All but two of us wanted to start their own businesses. I remember thinking how nuts they all were. I loved the idea of having a job, getting paid for doing what I love. It seemed so simple and so obvious (and so safe). As a designer, I helped corporate clients achieve workplace efficiencies and business goals. I created the spaces where my clients' employees and teams could show up to be their best and do their best. I loved my work. And then I found coaching—or rather, it found me. At a young age, I'd learned to trust the "signs" and synchronicities of life—especially when they showed up in patterns of three. (Ever have that happen?)

That's how it happened for me with coaching. Over the span of a week or so, "coaching" showed up in my life in various ways. I read about coaching in Oprah's magazine, and it seemed fascinating that people would pay coaches to help them. I saw it referenced in a book that mentioned how leaders were turning to coaches to create success. Then a team member shared an article and told me how coaching described my natural management style. There it was. A pattern of three.

I loved designing spaces to support people to show up as their best selves and do their best work. But I quickly realized that coaching was just helping people be their best no matter what space they were in. It was the core of what I loved. So, I trusted and began learning about this thing called "coaching" that I had never heard of before. That was back in 2002, and the industry was still relatively new.

I met coaches of all types—life purpose, relationship, and small-business coaches. I began researching what it meant to be a coach, learning that it was about supporting and inspiring clients to build on their capabilities and to overcome obstacles and barriers. That it was about helping clients tap into their full potential to achieve personal and professional goals. I went to a regional ICF (International Coaching Federation) conference with about 400 hundred coaches in attendance. *Wow!* I had found my people.

I began devouring everything I could about coaching. I hired a coach. I began taking coach training classes. Before long, I was dabbling as a coach myself, helping small-business

INTRODUCTION

owners reclaim the personal lives they had lost when they first turned their passions or hobbies into a business. Coaching was perfect as a hobby for me. I had the safety (and paycheck) that came with my job, which I still loved. Coaching fit nicely and neatly around that.

However, overachieving perfectionist that I was, I had been working fifty to sixty hours a week at my design job. The more I dabbled in coaching as a side gig, the fewer hours I worked at my day job (granted, I was still putting in forty to fifty or more hours while continuing to do high-quality design work). The owners of that firm could see the writing on the wall. They fired me (that's a story for another book). As I write those words, I can still feel the shock in my system. As a high-achieving perfectionist, I never get fired! Yet it happened.

The extreme fear from being fired spiraled me quickly into an irrational assessment of my life. I literally thought I was going to end up dead, naked, and lying in a gutter. I've never experienced fear like that since. After my close friend talked me off that ledge, I made a decision: *no one would ever be in charge of my future like that ever again!* I would take control of my own future. I would turn my hobby of coaching into a business.

Don't look now, Melinda, but you're an entrepreneur.

Once I made the decision to start my own business, I was on the fast track from hobbyist to amateur. I knew two things when I first made that commitment:

1. If I was going to ask people to pay good money to hire me as their coach, I had better be sure I could deliver what I promised.

2. If people were going to pay me, they needed to take me and my business seriously, which meant I had to take it seriously too.

So, I took it seriously. I learned everything I needed to know about this new endeavor and quickly advanced from amateur to professional.

In that unexpected moment of being fired, my life took a turn I never could have anticipated. The fear and shock I experienced propelled me onto a new path—one I hadn't planned for.

Fast-forward one year. I had a full roster of paying clients with a waiting list. I had already replaced my interior design salary through my coaching business income. Fast-forward a second year, and I started to pursue what would become my life's purpose—to help *other coaches* eliminate the burdens and distractions of their business so they could be their best and live their God-given potential. That was the birth of The Coaches Console, a multimillion-dollar coaching and software business that's generated over $20 million in revenue and is still growing and thriving today.

As of the writing of this book, I've spent almost twenty years coaching coaches—more than 120,000 coaches have been impacted by my work. And let's take it a bit further. The ICF's most recent 2023 survey states that the average coach practitioner works with an average of 12.2 clients at a time. That's not even total clients over their whole coaching career. That's just the number of clients at any one given time. So 120,000 coaches 12.2 clients per coach = 1.46 million clients who have received guidance from the coaches whose lives and businesses I've touched.

INTRODUCTION

All because I chose to face my fear that day I was fired and to become a professional coach. Talk about a ripple effect!

To Have Long-Term Success, You Need to Be a Professional

You'll notice that in my journey, I went through three distinct stages: hobbyist, amateur, and professional. It might be the same for you. And this book is your resource to get to that professional stage as quickly as possible.

Throughout the book, I'll use the phrase "professional coach." I'm not referring to the skills of coaching or to the certification of "Professional Coach" one can obtain. I'm referring to running your own coaching business in a thoroughly professional manner.

Many coaches get stuck in the amateur category for extended periods, often without realizing it, and without making significant progress or producing tangible results. They may consider themselves professionals, but their thoughts, behaviors, and actions don't align with genuine professionalism.

This book is for those who aspire to be true professionals. Because when that alignment happens, the journey flows and you become unstoppable.

Confidence and Professionalism

In my first book, *The Confident Coach*, I shared my Coaching Business Roadmap to Success (more of that in the "Pillar 8:

Implementing Business Operations" chapter of this book). That particular success path focuses on *what to do* behind the scenes to create a thriving, profitable coaching business. It's about what specific steps to take or not to take, and when to take them to turn your business into a well-oiled machine. That book's focus helps to reduce overwhelm and increase your confidence.

This book, on the other hand, focuses on *how to be* during your business-building journey. It's about how to think and behave in a professional manner while you're doing the tasks, taking the actions, and implementing the steps that create, organize, and streamline your business. It's about how you show up in every phase of your business journey evolution. When you know how to *be*, you can choose to move forward with your business in a way and at a pace that works for your lifestyle.

If you're just getting started (or thinking about getting into coaching), this book and the success path I outline will help you feel both confident and professional right out of the gate—even when you don't know what you don't know. If you're an established coach and have been at this for a while, this book will help you take yourself and your business to a new level—if that's what you want—without working harder, longer hours, and without sacrificing your lifestyle along the way.

Often, I hear that my coaching clients are afraid of success. They believe that if they're too successful, it will disrupt the already incredible parts of their lives, such as their current relationship with their spouse or time with their kids. They don't yet know how to *be* or what to *do*. They fear spiraling out of control and getting beaten down with overwhelm, so they dig in their heels out of fear, and hang out at the hobbyist or amateur level for far too long.

In reality, being a professional running your own coaching business is an invitation for you to step into the next greatest version of yourself and live your full potential.

Why Professionalism Is More Important Than Ever

Now is a great time to start or scale a coaching business. However, in order to succeed in today's market, you're going to have to work smarter as we're experiencing an intersection of three critical factors: a growing demand for coaching, evolving buyers, and a maturing industry.

A Growing Demand for Coaching

According to Ipsos and Pew Research Center surveys, around half of Americans report that they are reevaluating their life priorities and prioritizing a better work-life balance. There's a surge in people making positive lifestyle changes in *all* areas of their lives, even in the midst of global uncertainties. They are seeking professional support to create real change. You have a powerful part to play in this evolution with your coaching skills. *You* are the leader people turn to for help in navigating their lives.

Evolving Buyers

Clients are being extremely mindful about what or who they invest in, when they spend their money, and where they commit their time. They are now very much focused on the results they'll gain from hiring a coach.

Those investing in coaching are now asking, "*Why you?* Of the coaches I know, why should I hire *you* to be my coach? How are *you* uniquely qualified to help me create transformation and results in my life?"

The answer to that critical question goes beyond your coaching skills. Running a professional business will help you feel confident as a coach, and thus create a great experience for your clients to achieve results.

A Maturing Industry

The number of coaches in the world is higher than ever.

In a training I attended given by my colleague, Lisa Ann Edwards, she mapped out a trajectory of the number of coaches in the industry. As former head of Global Talent Management for Bill Gates's privately owned businesses, she has trained more than 10,000 coaches on how to measure, evaluate and demonstrate the monetary impact of coaching. In her research, she said, "Looking at the number of ICF certified coaches, in 2010 there were 17,000. In 2020 that number jumped to 31,000. Just three years later, in 2023 that number almost doubled to 60,000. If we continue following that trend, by 2030 there could be 128,000 ICF certified coaches."

INTRODUCTION

According to an ICF Global Coaching Study, revenue for the global coaching industry in 2023 was up 62 percent from 2019. In 2024, the industry is estimated to reach $20 billion, with PricewaterhouseCoopers reporting it to be the second-fastest growing sector in the world.

The upward trajectory can also be seen in online coaching platforms. In a recent study by business expert Luisa Zhou, her research found that in 2020, the online coaching market was nearly $2 billion. By 2028, her research shows this market size is projected to increase to $4.5 billion. Investors continue to create software platforms and develop apps to service both coaches and clients.

This increase in the number of coaches is matched by an increased demand for coaching. To make it attainable to get clients, launch, and grow a business in today's market, coaches need to answer two critical questions:

1. How do I put myself out there and succeed in a market where there are already so many coaches?
2. How will I get clients?

This book will guide you through what it takes to be a professional coach with a professional business that stands out in today's market, cultivating credibility, attracting high-paying clients, and creating a thriving business you love.

Let's get started on building the skills and competencies needed.

Navigating the Book
MAKING THE MOST OF YOUR BUSINESS ADVENTURE

> Move out of your comfort zone. You can only grow if you are willing to feel awkward and uncomfortable when you try something new.
> —Brian Tracy

To give you the best reading and learning experience, and the best business outcomes from this book, here are a few suggestions and recommendations. The next two chapters address fundamentals intended to establish a strong foundation and prepare you for the journey ahead. I recommend reading these chapters first and in order. However, for the eight chapters that address different pillars of professionalism, there's no need to approach these chapters in a linear manner.

Skip Around

You can certainly start at the beginning and read the whole book in order. I've drawn on my twenty years of coaching coaches in their businesses to create a natural flow. But if you find yourself struggling in a specific area, feel free to skip straight to that topic. Or if one of the topics feels easy for you to quickly implement, jump to that chapter and mark it off your list. Just be sure to circle back and read the remaining chapters, as they collectively form a complete picture of what it entails to be a professional running your own coaching business.

Implement As You Read

As you read, do the work! Each of the Pillar chapters and the Sustainability chapter include valuable **Going Pro Tips** as well as a **Going Pro Checklist**, making it simple to implement the strategies, tactics, and tips I've shared and making it easy to incorporate professionalism into your business.

Bring Your Whole Self

My students and community love the unique way I infuse Spirit into my business. At the end of each chapter, you'll find a section called the **Oracle Card Exercise**. This exercise draws on my favorite oracle deck, the Mystical Shaman Oracle deck by Colette Baron-Reid, Alberto Villoldo, and Marcela Lobos, which represents multiple ancient wisdom teachings and traditions. My father was a minister who preached, "one truth, many paths." In line with that idea, I've developed a ritual with this deck that helps me connect more deeply with Spirit to bring that which is greater than me into all that I do—my business included.

Daily, before sitting down at my computer to start my workday, I draw a card from this deck to receive guidance from Spirit (though you may refer to it by another label). The guidance might be helpful in navigating my day, figuring out how to handle a specific situation, or gaining insight related to something I may be stuck on. This practice helps me ground myself, welcoming in the magic and receiving guidance from both my intuition and from Spirit.

When I was first developing this ritual, my soul sister, Lindsay, taught me to ask a very powerful question when drawing oracle cards: "Why is this the perfect card for me right now?" Then I'd live into the question as a way to tap into my own intuition, strengthening my connection with Spirit.

I want to create this experience for you as well. I want you to save room for magic, and for specific messages the Universe might have for you as they relate to the content shared in the chapter material.

When I completed writing each chapter, I sat down at my altar and drew an oracle card for you, the reader, asking the Universe what message it wanted to convey to you about that chapter's topic. With Colette's blessing, I included the card I drew and its message in the Oracle Card Exercise section at the end of each chapter. I have listed the card name and card number from the deck and have included a portion of the message for you to contemplate. As each reader will interpret the message differently, I've also provided space for you to journal about why that particular card is the perfect card for you based on your current situations and circumstances.

If this is a practice you're accustomed to, enjoy. If working with oracle cards isn't something you've done (or maybe you haven't done it in relation to your business), I invite you to adopt a curiosity mindset and research what it's like. As with anything, take what works for you and leave the rest.

Do the Exercises for Thorough Integration

Do you remember your last holiday meal? Holiday meals are usually filled with our favorite foods, making it hard to resist getting seconds, even thirds, because it's all so delicious. What happens after that amazing meal? We're left stuffed and uncomfortable. It's necessary to take time and digest all that was just consumed.

It's the same when reading a book or experiencing anything amazing. For many, it is common to go from idea to idea, chapter to chapter without taking time to reflect and "digest." Constant consumption without taking a pause can keep your brain over-engaged, leading to exhaustion and burnout if you're not careful—even if the content is amazing.

But when you take a moment to pause and reflect on the ideas shared in each chapter, you integrate the learnings not only on an intellectual level, but also on emotional and spiritual levels. This pause is critical for thorough integration and easier implementation. It also creates space for new ideas to assimilate based on what you've just learned. You'll hear concepts differently; synchronicities will occur; insights from other sources will build on what you've just experienced.

At the end of each chapter, you'll find a **Favorite Frames** section designed to help create a pause. After this pause, write down your favorite frames so you can process and integrate the ideas, insights, and new learnings you've just read.

Your favorite frames are the phrases of the chapter you highlighted, gems that stood out for you, nuggets you want to remember, or key learnings you want to integrate. I learned this tool from Regena Thomashauer, a mentor who taught me the importance of reflecting on and remembering the highlights of an experience. I've since integrated these at the end of all my client calls, webinars, and events as a way to wrap up each session.

Follow the Create Without Burnout Cycle

For seven years, I was in a mastermind group with fifty other industry leaders, working to create our best lives while creating our best businesses. One of the members, Michelle Falzon, shared her Create Without Burnout model. As a strategic content and marketing expert who has helped her thought-leader clients generate in excess of $100 million through courses, events, books, and more, Michelle has studied what makes the difference between creators who thrive and continue to do their best work versus those who burn out or create things that fall short of their vision. When she shared her model, I knew immediately that it was going to be a game changer. I implemented it right away, and it transformed my life and business. I wasn't burned out, but the nuances within this cycle helped me to become even better at the work I was doing and love it even more. Michelle generously gave me permission to share her Create Without Burnout Cycle with you here:

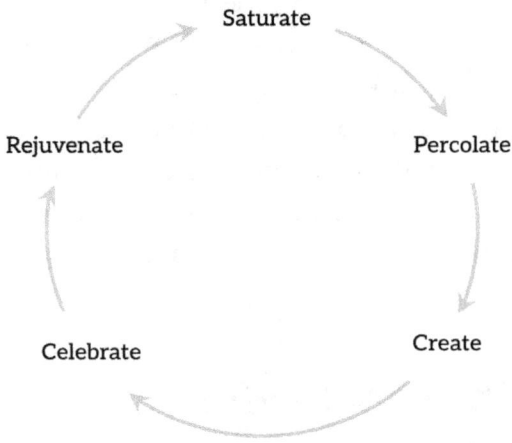

The Five Stages of the Create Without Burnout Cycle

Saturate: a phase of input where you're gathering information, researching, and learning.

Percolate: a moment to pause, step away, and engage in unrelated activities while your unconscious keeps making abstract and powerful progress on your idea.

Create: a stage for doing, writing, implementing, and action-taking.

Celebrate: a time to acknowledge whether you hit the goal or not.

Rejuvenate: a period for rest, renewal, rebuilding of your reserves.

Most people start at the Saturate phase and then jump immediately to Create, only to head straight back to Saturate, then to Create. This back-and-forth, back-and-forth is the fast path to burnout. However, when you can follow the cycle in her model and insert Percolate, Celebrate, and Rejuvenate—this is when creativity skyrockets and everything flows more effortlessly.

I applied this model to writing each chapter of *this* book. As a result, the art and process of writing was one that I savored, and the words flowed effortlessly. I fell in love with writing this book. I believe the same model can be just as impactful for you in reading it.

Reading each chapter is the Saturate phase, where you're taking in the knowledge and insights presented.

For the Percolate phase, the Oracle Card Exercise at the end of each chapter will help you in shifting your attention from the chapter content toward contemplating the material from a different perspective. I also suggest you step away from the content of the chapter, allowing what you've just taken in to simmer. This could be as simple as staring out the window for a few minutes or moving to a different project for a short period of time.

Then pick the book back up to that same chapter and Create—implementing the Going Pro Tips and Checklist items into your business, and capturing your favorite frames.

Once you complete the checklist, it's time to Celebrate. Acknowledge the progress you're making. Celebrate by calling a friend or a peer coach, or even taking a fun dance break.

Finally, it's time for a moment to Rejuvenate. As you complete a chapter, what is one thing you can do to refuel before moving on? Is it going for a walk, playing with your dog? Or maybe taking a jujitsu class, getting a massage, or enjoying a nap? Just make sure you're building up your reserves of joy and energy. From that place of being filled up, then you can move on to the next chapter. Enjoy the flow and process of stepping into your professionalism.

You'll also read in the chapter on Sustainability in Business toward the end of the book how to apply this same model to creating a sustainable and scalable business.

Being intentional about the way you read this book will help you assimilate the learnings quickly, implement at optimal levels, and find your flow in the process.

Let's get started!

Oracle Card Exercise
#6 The Blade

The Blade represents sharpness of the mind, body, and spirit. When aimed down to the ground, it anchors the power of the heavens on Earth. The blade can be a healing tool or a weapon. Wield it wisely, and it will transmit power, bestow initiations, cut energetic cords from the past, or sever toxic relationships. . . .

. . . Do not offer your blade in service to toxic emotions! You'll be faced with an even more disagreeable future. . . . Then use the blade with impeccable intention to cut the energetic cords that are tying you to the drama at hand. Set yourself free!

Why is this the perfect message for you, right now?

Take a few moments of quiet reflection time to journal what the message means to you:

_____

_____

_____

_____

Favorite Frames

Take a moment to write down your top takeaways, key learnings, aha moments, and insights that stood out the most. I know typically there are not a lot of insights within a "Navigating the Book" chapter, but use this as practice. By identifying these, you deepen your commitment to becoming a professional.

Here are some of my favorite frames to recap some of the key points in this chapter:

- Skip to the topics easiest to complete to make quick progress.
- Create space for messages from the Universe to intertwine magic and Spirit into Business.
- Be intentional about the way to read the book, focusing not just on completing it, but percolating on the concepts within each chapter.

Feel free to add your own favorite frames in the following space!

THE NATURAL EVOLUTION OF A COACHING BUSINESS

> Some people dream of success, while other people get up every morning and make it happen.
> —Wayne Huizenga

Imagine you're having a conversation with someone about your passion for coaching, and about your coaching business.

> If someone called you a hobbyist, how would you react?
>
> What if someone called you an amateur? What reaction would that elicit?
>
> Now, what if I called you a professional?

Often when I ask coaches these questions, the first two labels, especially amateur, are met with resistance and scoffs, *hmph*s, and defensiveness. They want to be professionals, right away. Before we dive into the distinctions among the three, it's important to debunk the bad rap associated with amateur.

The root word of *amateur* comes from Old French, *ameour*, meaning "one who loves." (I know, right?! I didn't realize that either.)

In contrast, when you look at today's definition of *amateur*, the Oxford Dictionary gives two meanings:

1. One who engages in a pursuit on an unpaid rather than professional basis.
2. A person who is incompetent or inept at a particular activity.

That first definition is closer to the root word meaning: you're doing an activity for love rather than money. But in today's culture, the second definition is more common. When someone describes you as an amateur, they're often saying you're incompetent. So it's natural to feel offended or put off, especially when they're talking about your passion, calling, and dreams.

But in reality, being an amateur is part of a natural and necessary progression on your way to being a professional coach.

Hobbyist → Amateur → Professional

None of these stages are necessarily good or bad. They're just different. And they each provide necessary ingredients on the journey.

The Journey to Professionalism Often Begins As a Hobbyist

You most likely started dabbling in coaching because you experienced a profound transformation in your own life, and you naturally wanted to start helping others to have a similar experience. Hobbyists do something strictly for personal pleasure. You coach for fun, make a few bucks as a side gig, and that's it. Any income becomes "fun money," if you make any income at all. You spend minimal time on coaching—as long as it's fun. Your hobby fits around your existing job and lifestyle.

For many coaches, right out of the gate they know they want to create a coaching business and jump straight past the hobbyist stage. If that's you, then great!

But if you're a hobbyist right now, you're ready to evolve to amateur if:

- The amount of time you're spending on coaching is no longer satisfying your desire for coaching.
- You realize that coaching is a much bigger calling.
- You're ready to make more money doing more of what you love.

The Evolution of Your Business Requires Time As an Amateur

For those that want to keep going beyond the hobbyist level, it's at the amateur level where they really start to gain traction and find out what kind of impact they can make. At the amateur level, they begin to understand what it could look like to have a business doing the thing they love.

Amateurs spend more time coaching than hobbyists. They have dedicated work hours and targets for the number of clients they want to coach. Setting intentions and goals for hours and clients, no matter how big or small, is what advances someone past the hobbyist level to become an amateur.

Where hobbyists don't place emphasis on making money at coaching, amateurs start to focus on generating revenue. While the income made as an amateur can be sporadic, it is often used to reinvest in the business or supplement an existing job/career.

Amateurs are learning and figuring things out. Business can feel a bit messy at this stage—it's supposed to. Market research is conducted, messaging is refined, packages and offers are piloted, and pricing is tested. These elements aren't nailed down just yet right out of the gate. The only way to know what works is to create, implement, test, review, and refine. The clarity gained as an amateur becomes a strong foundation for a professional business.

It's at this level that coaches start to build their brand, understand what type of person they can best coach, and expand their client base beyond the circles of people they already know. Some coaches stop here. And that's okay too. They're doing something they love and doing it well. They're spending a small amount of time on it and making some money.

Embracing the Amateur . . . For a While

When you first venture down the path of establishing and starting your business, it's natural that you'll spend a little bit of time in the amateur phase.

THE NATURAL EVOLUTION OF A COACHING BUSINESS

When I went back to the original meaning of an amateur and understood its meaning to be one who cultivates and participates in something they love but does not pursue it professionally, I had a new appreciation of the word. During the early days of your business, it's important and freeing to embrace your amateur status, not resist it.

Embracing the amateur:

- You're willing to learn about something that's new with a commitment to do it well, even when it's awkward at first. You value progress over perfection.
- You love doing something, so you dedicate a decent amount of time to doing it.
- You're comfortable acknowledging that you're new at something as you learn and grow.

Resisting the amateur:

- You misinterpret the inconsistencies with marketing, getting clients, and generating income in the early stages of your business to mean you're doing something wrong.
- You're quick to give up or shift directions.
- You feel overly concerned with what people will say or think about you.

THE PROFESSIONAL COACH

- You develop a fear-based belief that being new and inexperienced means people won't trust you or hire you.

It's only when you resist the amateur and get *stuck* at the amateur level that it starts to feel bad. When you're out of alignment with how you perceive yourself, that creates an internal tug of war, making it hard to make any progress in your business.

On average, new coaches will spend three to six months in this amateur phase, maybe even upwards of a year if they're balancing a full-time job or other family responsibilities on top of trying to start their business. That's normal. The faster you can embrace the amateur stage, the more quickly you'll advance to that of a professional.

It's always shocking how many new coaches I work with think they're supposed to magically know how to operate as a professional and immediately have a successful business right away. You don't! But if you want to become a professional, you need to consistently work toward that goal.

Let's turn to golf for some insight. Even if you're not a golfer (I'm not), it's one of the sports where being an amateur is equally as acceptable as being a pro. Golf amateurs know they can't just jump straight to pro. They have to spend time as an amateur, gaining practice, building skills, and dipping their toe into tournaments.

"Oh, poor Tiger Woods, he's only an amateur," said no one ever. Instead, while Woods was an amateur, folks (including himself and his father) talked about how he was improving, they showcased areas he was focusing on in his practice sessions,

THE NATURAL EVOLUTION OF A COACHING BUSINESS

and they commented about how amazing he was going to be once he did go pro. It was a natural part of the journey.

We have to let go of any mistaken beliefs that being an amateur is undesirable, is bad, or makes us less than capable. Instead, adopt a mindset focused on continuous improvement. Here are some resiliency mindsets to embrace as you make your way through the early amateur phase:

1. **Focus on the Process, Not the Results:** Instead of fixating solely on outcomes, concentrate on personal development and skill enhancement in the early stage. Let learning be okay. Acknowledge that progress takes time, and each lesson learned is a step toward improvement.

2. **Be Curious:** Embrace the learning process with a sense of curiosity, and find joy in the journey itself. Appreciate the improvements you make, and savor the experiences. Remember that every professional was once an amateur who faced challenges.

3. **Build a Support System:** Surround yourself with a positive and supportive community of fellow coaches, mentors, and friends. Sharing experiences and challenges with others who understand your journey can provide encouragement and motivation.

Remember, the amateur phase is part of the natural progression toward operating professionally. By focusing on personal growth, welcoming the learning experience, and being curious, coaches who are currently amateurs can navigate the challenges and maintain their enthusiasm for doing what they love along the way to becoming professionals.

It's time to evolve from amateur to professional when you know you want to:

- Consistently work with more clients than you currently have.
- Generate more income and profit that's consistent and reliable.
- Make a bigger impact through your services.
- Experience more ease in your business and life.

Going Pro

If you think coaching could be a lucrative business for you and you're ready to live your full potential as a coach, welcome to the club! This road is not for the faint of heart, though. There's a lot involved in being a professional coach running a professional business.

Not to worry. If you've evolved beyond the ranks of amateur (or are ready to), then I'm glad this book has made its way into your hands. The remainder of this book will dive into the definitions, nuances, and key components necessary to adopt a professional approach in starting, launching, and running your business.

Just about every coach I encounter stresses the driving need to be professional. When I ask them why that is so important, I hear answers such as, "I want people to see me as credible," "I want them to trust me and take my business seriously," "I want them to hire me and buy my packages," and "I want them to feel comfortable recommending me."

In my twenty years of experience, many of my clients have gone on to become extremely successful coaches. I interviewed some of these success stories, asking, "What does it mean to be professional?" There was a variety of answers. Being professional, they said, means being competent, qualified, skillful, thorough, dedicated, reliable, respected, knowledgeable, and organized. All of these qualities describe *how* you show up as a coach inside your business.

Some coaches shared more tangible criteria. A professional shows up to appointments prepared and on time, responds in a timely manner to clients' questions and assignments, and sets clear boundaries with clients around expectations. For others, it was important that a professional receive a certification and follow a code of ethics. One coach said she'd gleaned from her corporate days that professionalism is not just about the services provided, but also how the client feels when they are inside of your business, and how you build your brand's ethos.

According to the IRS, a professional business is one actively trying to earn a profit (while the amateur's focus is on generating top-line revenue and the hobbyist's is enjoying the little bit of pocket change it may encounter from time to time).

So how do *you* define what it means to be a professional running your own coaching business?

THE PROFESSIONAL COACH

Take a few moments and in the space below, journal what "being professional" means to you.

_____

_____

_____

_____

Now, on a scale of 1–5, rank how competent you currently feel at each of the things you've listed (with 1 being "it barely exists in my current business" and 5 being "I am totally competent and confident in this area").

The War of Art author, Steven Pressfield, has an especially interesting description of how the differences between amateurs and pros show up in their behavior, actions, and habits: "The difference between an amateur and a professional is in their habits. An amateur has amateur habits. A professional has professional habits. We can never free ourselves from habit. But we can replace bad habits with good ones."

It is important when pursuing professionalism to have a general idea about how far you want your business to grow, and what you are willing to do to create it. Treating your business as a hobby will bring you hobby results (if you have a business at all). You will go from client to client without ever finding any stability. Maybe you'll have a lot of fun doing it. Maybe that's enough for you. But maybe not.

As an amateur, you will already be doing quite a bit of what is required to succeed and make a good living. But you will never evolve to become a professional unless you take the actions that professionals take. And only someone who acts as a professional can expect to be paid like one.

Oracle Card Exercise
#41 The Rainbow

. . . In the Himalayas, the rainbow body is seen as the full realization of our essence. The Rainbow also represents the bridge between the physical and spiritual worlds. . . . When the rainbow appears, it is an affirmation that all is well and that you are in the right relationship with Spirit.

Why is this the perfect message for you, right now, as it relates to this chapter?

Take a few moments of quiet reflection time to journal what the message means to you:

_____

_____

_____

_____

Favorite Frames

Take a moment to write down your top takeaways, key learnings, aha moments, and insights that stood out the most. By identifying these, you deepen your commitment to becoming a professional.

Here are some of my favorite frames to recap some of the key points in this chapter:

- *Amateur* doesn't have to be a bad label. It's just that we don't want to get stuck at this level if we want to make a bigger impact in this world.
- Being a professional coach is about *how to be* while taking the necessary actions on your business-building journey.
- The amateur's focus is on top-line revenue. The professional's focus is on profit.

Feel free to add your own favorite frames in the following space!

THE PATH TO PROFESSIONALISM

*Perseverance is not a long race;
it is many short races one after the other.*
—Walter Elliot

Once you decide that doing coaching just for the fun of it doesn't satisfy your inner drive and calling, you're well on your way. Next, there are eight pillars that will allow you to develop the competence for running your own coaching business in a thoroughly professional manner.

Pillar 1: Expanding Commitment and Dedication

Pillar 2: Defining Work Ethic

Pillar 3: Creating Your Unique Value Proposition

Pillar 4: Establishing Accountability for Outcomes

Pillar 5: Designing Delivery of Client Support

Pillar 6: Setting Professional Pricing

Pillar 7: Managing Business Finances

Pillar 8: Implementing Business Operations

The Eight Pillars of Professionalism

A Comprehensive Overview to Run Your Business in a Professional Manner

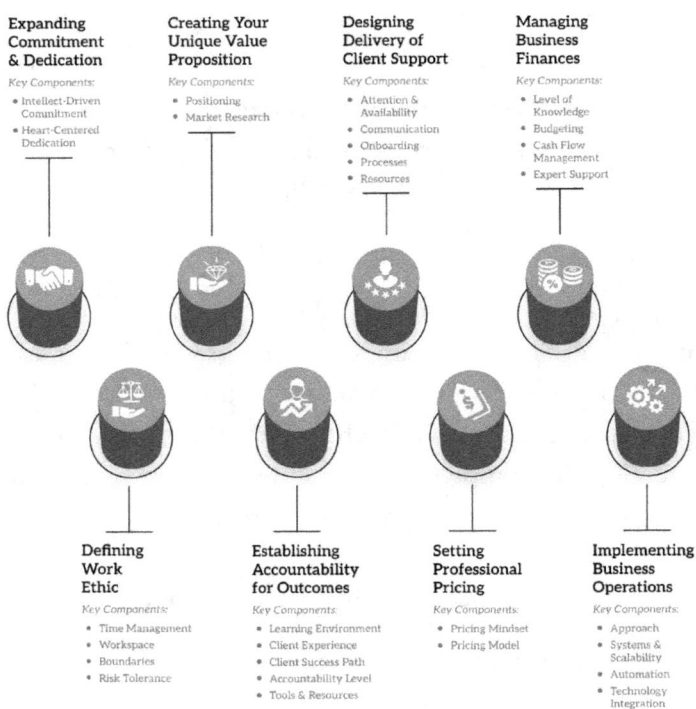

The Eight Pillars of Professionalism

Visit the Additional Resources in the back of the book to download a copy of this Blueprint.

The following chapters will provide details, mindset shifts, and exercises to master each of these pillars. For now, here's an overview of the role each pillar plays in building your professionalism.

Pillar 1: Expanding Commitment and Dedication

This is where your journey as an amateur begins to shift. As an amateur, your only commitment is to doing what you love. But to become a professional coach, you'll need to expand your commitment to the work and demonstrate your dedication to maintaining progress no matter what obstacles may appear. Commitment is often made with the head, and it comes with a sense of responsibility that is strengthened through tasks and actions. Dedication is made with the heart, and it is driven by one's passion in pursuit of the thing they're committed to.

Key Components:

1. Intellect-Driven Commitment
2. Heart-Centered Dedication

Pillar 2: Defining Work Ethic

When people discuss the concept of work ethic, they're often talking about working hard and earning a reward. In this section, however, I'm referring to a personal set of standards for acceptable behaviors in business—everything from your core values to the environment you work in, the hours you set, and the boundaries you establish. A good work ethic also involves determining structure, organization, time management, and tolerance for risk.

Key Components:

1. Time Management
2. Workspace
3. Boundaries
4. Risk Tolerance

Pillar 3: Creating Your Unique Value Proposition

Your Unique Value Proposition (UVP) describes the benefits your business offers to the customers who invest in your services. It's a simple statement that summarizes why a customer should select you and your offerings over the other coaches in the market.

With new clients asking, "Why should I hire you to be my coach and help me achieve results?" your lived experience—all the years of overcoming adversity to find success, all the trainings, the jobs, the specialties you bring to the table—has equipped you to answer. You just have to be bold and say *yes* to being authentically yourself. That unique part of yourself, in combination with your skill set, is exactly what will resonate with those you're meant to serve.

Key Components:

1. Positioning
2. Market Research

Pillar 4: Establishing Accountability for Outcomes

Coaches should be held accountable for establishing a supportive environment, orchestrating great experiences that guide clients through their journeys, determining the appropriate accountability level for clients to attain results, and equipping them with the essential tools and resources to maintain momentum toward desired outcomes.

By taking shared accountability for outcomes, you demonstrate your commitment, your reliability, and your dedication to helping clients achieve their goals.

Key Components:

1. Learning Environment
2. Client Experience
3. Client Success Path
4. Accountability Level
5. Tools and Resources

Pillar 5: Designing Delivery of Client Support

With the evolved buyer becoming more savvy and demanding results from their investment, supporting clients to achieve real outcomes goes beyond the coaching session. There is much to consider when structuring how you'll support your clients on their journey of transformation.

You'll need to decide how accessible you'll be outside of the coaching session; how you'll structure your packages, program, and services; the resources you'll offer for deeper accountability; and the way you'll communicate with and onboard your clients. These are some of the overlooked professional competencies to be integrated into the fulfillment and delivery of your client support. Not to worry; we'll explore each of these in the chapter dedicated to this aspect of professionalism.

Key Components:

1. Attention
2. Availability
3. Communication
4. Onboarding
5. Processes
6. Resources

Pillar 6: Setting Professional Pricing

Pricing is often a topic that can derail a coach's business-building journey. As a hobbyist, you didn't have to spend too much time determining what clients paid you—if it was enough, if it was too much. Heck, for many hobbyists, their clients don't pay them at all. As an amateur, your focus was primarily on testing various price points and offers.

But when you want to establish any level of consistent, reliable income (no matter the amount) generated by your coaching services, pricing can get tricky fast if you're not paying attention.

Setting professional pricing doesn't have to be hard or triggering when you know what goes into it. It's when you let your fears determine your prices that it goes awry.

Key Components:

1. Pricing Mindset
2. Pricing Model

Pillar 7: Managing Business Finances

When making the decision to run your own business, no matter how big or small, understanding simple finances is important. Many can get intimidated and overlook this part of their business, leading to bigger financial headaches down the road. But finance isn't as complicated as it seems. It's just uncharted territory for a new business owner. Managing basic business finances is necessary, even if you don't like doing it, and we're going to break it down into simple tasks.

Key Components:

1. Level of Knowledge
2. Budgeting
3. Cash Flow Management
4. Expert Support

Pillar 8: Implementing Business Operations

A significant differentiation between a hobbyist, an amateur, and a professional lies in their approach to organizing and optimizing the back end of their business. The manner in which you implement and streamline your back end will create either overwhelm or an effortless flow.

Key Components:

1. Approach
2. Systems and Scalability
3. Automation
4. Technology Integration

Rating the Pillars

If I were working privately with you to review your business, I'd ask the following questions to determine which pillar would be a good starting point for you to focus on, which would create the most momentum, and what sequence would be ideal to follow.

If your answers to the following questions include some yeses and some nos sprinkled throughout each of the different pillars, that tells me you're just beginning to get your business started or that you've been jumping around in your business setup. There are probably gaps, holes, and missing elements that are needed to shore up your confidence and professionalism (which we'll cover in the following chapters).

Rate your professionalism by answering the following questions:

Pillar 1: Expanding Commitment and Dedication

    Y | N   Is your coaching business one of your top three priorities?

    Y | N   Have you created your "*Why* I Started My Coaching Business" statement?

Pillar 2: Defining Work Ethic

    Y | N   Have you identified the amount of time you're able to put toward your business?

Y | N   Is there an established, dedicated work space for you to work on/in your business?

Pillar 3: Creating Your Unique Value Proposition

Y | N   Have you conducted market research?

Y | N   Are you clear in describing your ideal client's challenges and desired results?

Y | N   Do you feel confident putting yourself out there and talking about your services?

Pillar 4: Establishing Accountability for Outcomes

Y | N   Do your clients have a secure place where they can easily access communications, tools, and resources throughout the coaching relationship?

Y | N   Is there a clear Client Success Path mapped out for clients to reference?

Pillar 5: Designing Delivery of Client Support

Y | N   Do you provide coaching and support beyond the coaching sessions?

Y | N   Is there an automated onboarding sequence in place for new clients?

Pillar 6: Setting Professional Pricing

Y | N   Do you have at least two offers created?

Y | N   Are you offering result-based packages?

Pillar 7: Managing Business Finances

    Y | N Do you have separate business and personal bank accounts?

    Y | N Do you review both budget and cash flow reports weekly or monthly?

Pillar 8: Implementing Business Operations

    Y | N Are you automating redundant, behind-the-scenes tasks for efficiency?

    Y | N Do you have a simple, integrated technology platform to manage your business and help you and your clients be organized?

A Quick Check-In: Are You an Amateur or a Professional?

Don't just give a knee-jerk answer. As you progress on your business-building journey, I want to make sure you're in total alignment with how you're perceiving yourself so you can accelerate your results. There's nothing worse than the overwhelm caused by the misalignment of your self-perceptions and actions.

So many coaches *think* they're professionals, but they're not *acting* like professionals. Their actions, and habits, speak louder than the way they see or think of themselves and their business.

As you read through the pillars in the subsequent chapters, be honest with yourself about which description best describes how you've been showing up in your business, making it clearer where alignment can occur, and improvements can be made for rapid growth.

Moving Through the Pillars

You can proceed through this book in one of three ways:

The Foundation Experience: For the first "no" you come to in the rating assessment above, that is the pillar you should focus on first for maximum impact.

The Quick Win Experience: Which pillar seems the easiest for you to complete? Start there so you can gain quick wins and build early momentum.

The Sequential Experience: Start with Pillar 1 and go in the sequence I've presented. You may find that you've already completed some elements in different pillars, but it will help build confidence knowing you've quickly reviewed those key components and are all set in that part of your business.

Ultimately, it doesn't matter what sequence you complete the pillars in. What matters is that you visit all the pillars and address each of the key components discussed in the upcoming chapters.

A Word of Caution

Don't leave exercises unfinished. While it may seem easier to work on just one thing from one pillar, then move on, that only fuels a reactionary, sporadic approach. You can go through the pillars in any order, but once you've started working on a pillar, see it through.

The final destination of your journey is the one you're diligently working toward, striving for, and dreaming of: becoming a Professional Coach with a *real* business that you can feel proud of.

Whether you are just now embarking on this path, have begun to embrace the professional approach in some areas, or have covered most aspects and just need a few refinements, you now have a path to success that lays out a comprehensive overview of what might be missing, what you might have overlooked, where there are gaps, and where your focus should lie.

Oracle Card Exercise
#45 The Seer

The Seer represents the capacity to reach beyond the obvious details, into the Hidden Realms where information is available to those with the discernment to perceive it. . . . The Seer knows truth, always seeks truth beyond all else, and sees reality as it truly is without judgment. . . . He represents the power of clarity and being able to recognize patterns.

The Seer has arrived now to challenge you to get out of denial and begin telling yourself the truth about your situation. Wishful thinking will not make your desires happen when you're refusing to see things as they are. The truth may hurt, but it will set you free to claim the bounty that is waiting for you to notice it. . . .

Why is this the perfect message for you, right now, as it relates to this chapter?

Take a few moments of quiet reflection time to journal what the message means to you:

_____
_____
_____
_____

Favorite Frames

Take a moment to write down your top takeaways, key learnings, aha moments, and insights that stood out the most. By identifying these, you deepen your commitment to becoming a professional.

Here are some of my favorite frames to recap some of the key points in this chapter:

- Eight key pillars develop professionalism, which is not something that just happens but is done with intentional action.

THE PATH TO PROFESSIONALISM

- Rating the pillars quickly reveals gaps, holes, and missing elements that are needed to shore up confidence and professionalism.
- The oracle card drawn challenges us to get out of denial and tell the truth about the situation—revealing the greatest opportunity for growth.

Feel free to add your own favorite frames in the following space!

Pillar 1
EXPANDING COMMITMENT AND DEDICATION

> Most people fail not because of a lack of desire,
> but because of a lack of commitment.
> —Vince Lombardi

Seventeen years ago, I sat at my desk looking at the stack of bills that I had shoved into a drawer, wondering, *How did I get so behind in my finances?*

I had made a lot of money quickly when I first launched my coaching business. In just six months, I'd made up for my lost corporate salary in coaching income. I even had a waiting list of clients ready to work with me. But then something changed when I launched The Coaches Console.

In the early years of launching that second business, I got myself deep in debt. I was normally meticulous about managing my money, but this time I found myself in new territory. I'd thought, since my first business was financially thriving within six months, the same thing would happen with The Coaches Console. But as it turned out, the revenue was minuscule for the first several years. I kept telling myself, *this is what's required when you're building and launching a software business* (which I had never done before). I kept thinking that, at any moment, something would change. But in those first few years, it didn't. Since I didn't adjust my lifestyle, I went deeper and deeper into debt.

Eventually, I found myself standing in front of an ATM inserting a credit card to withdraw funds at a 25 percent interest rate, just to be able to pay my mortgage. That was enough to break the cycle of denial.

I opened each envelope I had stuffed in drawers. I created a spreadsheet that showed all the debt in one location. I couldn't believe it. I shared the document with my business partner. She was shocked, but very understanding and supportive. I shared it with my coach, and he was non-judgmental too. I then scheduled a lunch with my dad to share it with him.

Now, here's what you need to know about my dad. He and my mom are my two biggest true believers: loving, supportive, always telling me that anything is possible. I knew that my dad would support me even in my mess, and that he'd have great ideas to help me turn things around.

But when I shared the situation with him over lunch and showed him the spreadsheet, he looked over it quietly for a few brief moments. He then, as only dads can do, slid his glasses to the tip of his nose, looked over the top rims, and said, "Melinda, it's simple. Your outgo is more than your income. You can't do this; you just need to get a job."

What?!?!? My dad had just ignored and dismissed my hard-fought dreams and told me to go get a job? That was the last thing I'd thought he would say. I shoved my chair away from the table, stood up, and said, "Oh yeah?! F&#%

PILLAR 1: EXPANDING COMMITMENT AND DEDICATION

that! Watch this!" I headed straight home and got to work on my business, figuring out new ways to make money without having to get a job or go deeper into debt. That was the day my commitment and dedication to my business catapulted. For the first time (in relation to launching The Coaches Console), I truly became a business owner and took my dream seriously.

As I looked deeper, I realized that I had an amateur level of commitment keeping me in a place of comfort, even when we weren't getting sign-ups or generating revenue. I was only focusing on the parts of the business I felt competent in, like working on the features in the Coaches Console System and supporting existing users in the software, but I was shying away from areas I wasn't familiar with, like marketing and sales. I was staying busy for the sake of being busy, thinking, *If I'm constantly spending time on the business, no one can argue I'm not giving it my all, even if we're not getting results.*

The wake-up call at that lunch with my dad took my commitment to a whole new level. I took on a "do whatever it takes" attitude. This made it easier to dive into new, unchartered territory. I immediately started learning everything I could about different ways I could find clients and generate money.

I went from blaming external factors for why results weren't happening, to taking full responsibility in making sure they did happen, no matter what.

Now that I have the gift of hindsight (and now that The Coaches Console is a multimillion-dollar business), I know my dad was not being a naysayer or dismissing my dreams.

He was simply sharing a solution with deep love, offering a way to turn that situation around as quickly as possible. Today, my dad is still one of my greatest heroes and biggest supporters of my business and my dreams. It just turned out that in that moment he was wrong: I didn't need a job. I needed more commitment to my business.

Remember, being an amateur isn't bad. It's a necessary phase. But it's imperative that you keep moving forward into the professional phase. If you remain in the comfort of the amateur phase too long, you'll start to become overwhelmed and frustrated with yourself and your business—or even go into debt like me.

When beginning the path toward becoming a professional coach, an important first step is to expand your commitment beyond that of an amateur and demonstrate your dedication.

Key Components to Expanding Commitment and Demonstrating Dedication

Let's explore important differences in how amateurs and professionals approach this pillar. Understanding these distinctions can significantly inform your growth in this area.

1. Intellect-Driven Commitment
   - *Amateurs* may lack the same level of intellectual commitment to their pursuits as professionals. They often engage in their activities as

part-time endeavors, and their commitment can vary.
  - *Professionals* consistently take actions to develop and grow their business. They understand that success requires a high level of responsibility, and they are willing to invest significant time and effort to achieve their goals.
2. Heart-Centered Dedication
  - *Amateurs* are often more sporadic and less focused due to part-time engagement and varying motivations.
  - *Professionals* tend to demonstrate unwavering passion, treating their business as a priority and primary occupation and making necessary choices to achieve their long-term goals.

The Scale of Commitment

It's your level of commitment that decides the level of success possible.

Take a few moments to paint the picture of what your commitment has looked like thus far. On a scale of 1–10, with 1 being "Nah, I'm not really committed" and 10 being "I'm all in, baby, and not looking back," how committed have you been to operating in a professional manner?

What's your number? Quick, say the number that's already come to mind. Don't overthink it. Whatever number comes up for you, remember: it's not bad, it's not a judgment.

It's just what is true for you in this particular moment.

Often when I ask coaches this, I immediately get a resounding "I'm a 10!!!" But when we dig a little deeper, it's clear they're making decisions in a way that demonstrates a lack of commitment—just like I once did, thinking I could get away with committing only to what I was already good at. They're enthusiastic. But that's not enough on its own.

Enthusiasm is not a commitment. Enthusiasm is a feeling. Commitment is what you actually do. Commitment is cultivated through the intellect, and it's rooted in a sense of responsibility. It requires a willingness to dedicate consistent time, show up fully even when you don't feel like it or want to, and be uncomfortable. We have to get profoundly comfortable with the discomfort of being an entrepreneur. Typically, enthusiasm is only present when things are going well. When obstacles appear or challenges arise, often enthusiasm turns into feelings of frustration. Relying only on your enthusiasm and excitement for what's possible will take you only about two to three weeks into the business-building journey before your old habits and patterns kick in.

Lack of commitment is the biggest reason why New Year's resolutions fail more often than they succeed. Researchers suggest that only 9 percent of Americans who make resolutions complete them, with 23 percent giving up by the end of the first week.

So let me ask you again. On a scale of 1–10, how committed have you been up to this point?

If you're a 5 or less, chances are you're not ready to go pro. There might be some soul-searching needed to help you

PILLAR 1: EXPANDING COMMITMENT AND DEDICATION

better understand exactly what's important to you about being a coach—and more importantly, about having your own coaching business and operating in a professional manner.

During a conversation with a gentleman several years ago, after reviewing everything included in our signature program to support him in achieving success, his response was, "So, Melinda, you're basically removing all of my excuses for why I'm not moving forward." You would think that was a good thing. But it turned out, he was at about a 4 or 5 on the commitment scale. Our conversations helped him clarify what he was (and was not) willing to commit to. The concept of a successful coaching business was attractive to him, but his commitment level didn't match the desire. Like many coaches who get excited about the idea of being a successful coach but lack the necessary commitment, he remained stuck in that same spot of ambivalence for years—he wanted to be successful as a coach, but he wasn't willing to do the work. And unfortunately, there was nothing I could do to help him overcome that particular obstacle. When commitment isn't there, change is not going to happen.

When I asked another coach about her level of commitment, she came to realize that her priority was actually to spend as much time as possible on her boat with her grandkids. She thought having a coaching business would be great (after all, she loved coaching). But through this exercise, she became really clear on what was most important to her—her grandkids. She remained a hobbyist and was able to be very involved with her family.

So if you're a 5 or less, pursuing professionalism is most likely not for you. That's okay. You can put this book down, enjoy the hobby of coaching, and focus on pursuing everything else that matters in your life.

On the other hand, if you're a 10, you're completely ready for all the insights and strategies in the chapters that lie ahead. When I think of a commitment level of 10, I always remember Margarita. She was a mother of three kids (all under the age of five). She was a caretaker for her husband. And she was launching her business (while she was pregnant with their next child). Nothing was stopping her from pursuing her passion. Her solid commitment level in conjunction with her strong enthusiasm created clarity around organizing herself and managing her time based on her priorities.

Most people, however, fall somewhere between a 6 and a 9. If that's you, what would it take for you to be a 10? Before you answer this for yourself, let's have a look at what people often don't understand about commitment.

Commitment is not a one-and-done, static statement that is made and then forgotten about. Only by committing to your practice *every day* do you demonstrate true commitment.

What's more, your commitment is often to something that is brand-new, a goal or dream that hasn't yet become a reality. In order to make it a reality, you have to take uncomfortable action daily—your commitment level must lie outside your comfort level.

Commitment requires habit changes (which the rest of the chapters will help you accomplish), so your commitment

PILLAR 1: EXPANDING COMMITMENT AND DEDICATION

can't solely be "I'm committed to being a professional coach," "I'm committed to helping others," or "I'm committed to creating a successful business." Those are your goals. Commitment is what helps you reach them.

Most coaches and leaders do support their clients in creating a commitment to an outcome. But what really accelerates your success, especially through all the obstacles and challenges that will arise, is to commit to *how* you're going to show up while pursuing that goal.

Try saying this out loud:

> "I'm committed to being who I need to be, and doing what needs to be done for my dreams to become a reality—even if it's uncomfortable."

How did that feel? Did you believe yourself? Do you think you can follow through today, and tomorrow, and three months from now when you're working on tedious business tasks and you don't feel like it?

If so, you have an unwavering commitment, and your end goal will be inevitable.

Let's go back to that other question. If you are a 6–9 on that scale of commitment, what would it take for you to be a 10?

_____

_____

_____

_____

Your *Why* Can Fuel Your Commitment

Your *why* describes all the reasons why you desire to be a great coach with a thriving, professional business. When you feel confident as a coach, when you have a successful and profitable coaching business, and when you're receiving amazing testimonials from your clients, what will that new reality allow you to do, be, or have?

Sometimes, your *why* will also include all the ways your life would be worse if you *didn't* make this change and your goals and dreams went unrealized.

Ask yourself, "Where will I be in six months if my business goals don't become a reality?" The answers to that uncomfortable question can also serve as fuel for your *why*.

Your *why* is your beacon. As with anyone learning any new skill or competence, you will experience times when you fall down, when mistakes are made, when obstacles appear. I can give you inspiring quotes about each of those:

> "It doesn't matter how many times you get knocked down, but how many times you get up."
> —Vince Lombardi

> "The only real mistake is the one from which we learn nothing."
> —Henry Ford

> "Obstacles are opportunities in disguise."
> —Deepak Chopra

PILLAR 1: EXPANDING COMMITMENT AND DEDICATION

But inspiring quotes will take you only so far. It's your *why*—your commitment to yourself, your business, and your passions—that you'll reach for when things get messy, tough, or tricky. In order to become the best version of yourself, you'll need an unwavering spirit.

After hitting my stride with my coaching business, I was riding with a friend one afternoon and began to hear a voice whispering phrases in my head. Being the daughter of a preacher, I was familiar with receiving messages from the Divine and knew to listen. I pulled a napkin out of the glove compartment and began writing down the phrases coming to me.

I didn't understand what they meant at first or what I was supposed to do about the message. A short time later it became clear. The message on the napkin was guidance for me to help coaches "eliminate the burdens and distractions" of business so they could "live their God-given potential." I knew that was how my unique gifts could serve coaches to help them make an impact on the world. The more coaches I could help be successful at coaching more people, the more people there would be being their best and living their full, God-given potential.

That was the spark of The Coaches Console. Knowing nothing about the world of software or web-based platforms at the time (remember, this was in 2004, before Software as a Service was even a phrase), I knew it was going to take a solid commitment to pursue this calling. I framed my napkin and hung it prominently in my home office, so I saw it every morning before I sat down to my computer. This consistent reminder of my *why* helped my commitment remain steady and the dedication to my passion strong.

I know not everyone will hear their *why* like I did. How do you define a strong, solid *why*? Try this exercise that I call the Stair Step to Your *Why*.

Fill in the blanks:

1. Why is starting your business important to you?

_____

2. Why is {answer to #1} important to you?

_____

3. Why is {answer to #2} important to you?

_____

4. Keep going up the stairs until you can't answer the question anymore.

_____

PILLAR 1: EXPANDING COMMITMENT AND DEDICATION

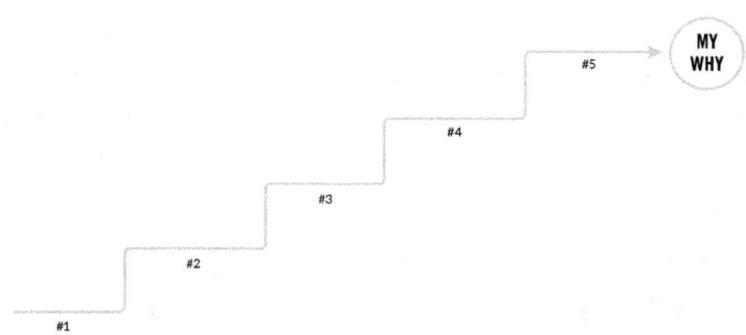

Stair Step to Your Why Exercise

Here's my example:

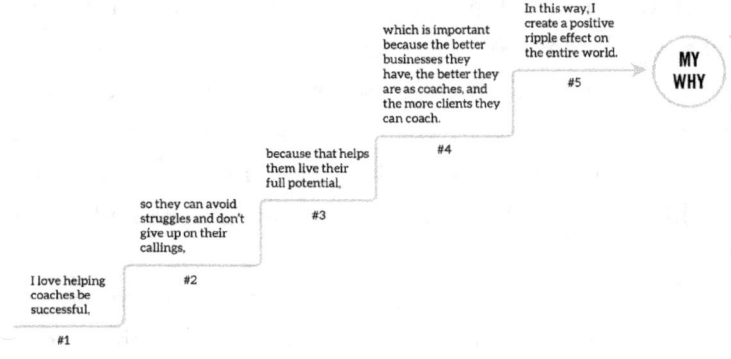

Different Degrees of Commitment

Commitment is unique to each person. The ways in which I act out my commitment level or what fuels my commitment level is going to be different from yours. That's okay. Let's paint the picture of your unique commitment level at various degrees:

> What does 100 percent commitment look like? Who are you being when you're 100 percent committed? What are you doing? What actions are you taking? What thoughts are you thinking? What are you saying? What are you not doing?
>
> What does 75 percent commitment look like?
>
> What does 50 percent commitment look like?

You're probably asking, "Melinda, why would I paint the picture of being only 75 percent committed or 50 percent committed if I'm supposed to be 100 percent committed all the time?" I know—strange, right?

When you can describe what lower levels of commitment look and sound like, it'll be easier to catch yourself when you start wavering—when your enthusiasm may still feel like you're at 100 percent, but your actions and words have faltered.

When you're describing 100 percent, don't aim for perfection. Commitment is different from perfection. In don Miguel Ruiz's book *The Four Agreements*, the fourth agreement is, "Always do your best." I remember I had a significant aha moment when I read this: *Your best today may look very different from your best yesterday, or tomorrow.* All of a sudden, my perfectionism tendencies softened, and I could lean into focusing on doing my best in any given moment.

Your Business Must Be a Priority

Just as your enthusiasm for coaching can taint your commitment levels, it can also wreak havoc on your priorities. It's not uncommon for amateurs to feel like everything is both urgent and necessary. When you clarify your priorities, you're better positioned to make conscious choices in support of your long-term goals.

I always ask a new coach to show me their calendar. Consistent blocks of time scheduled into the calendar to work *on* their business—strategic planning, product creation, process development, and other revenue-generating activities—reflect a commitment to their professional development. I also look for regular blocks of time added to the schedule to work *in* their business, executing the tasks in front of them—checking their inbox, facilitating discovery sessions, making client calls, and doing administration tasks like bookkeeping. Finally, I look for specific blocks of time to "work" *off* their business—taking breaks, going on vacation, engaging in rejuvenating activities—to build personal resilience.

If I don't see these on your calendar, then it's time for a heart-to-heart. It's easy to be busy for the sake of being busy, and often you're busy with the wrong activities. Time-blocking is a great time management method that provides guidelines for how to organize your day and stay focused. Intentionally leveraging time-blocking can help organize your schedule for effective outcomes and keep your business a priority.

What you schedule is what you prioritize. Your enthusiasm will have you thinking you're clear on your priorities, while what you spend your time on says otherwise. On several occasions, I've reviewed my clients' calendars only to find them filled with a wide range of appointments not business related—taking kids to sporting practices, working a part-time job, traveling for vacations, caring for other family members, and doing other hobby projects. It's not that those are bad or shouldn't be on your schedule. What I didn't see in those instances was any time devoted to their business. As a result, everything else took priority, leaving no time for business activities. They were saying things like, "when my schedule frees up, then I'll focus on my business."

Calendars can quickly reveal if there are too many priorities (the schedule is filled with other stuff besides business activities), or conflicting priorities (the schedule is filled with overlapping activities), or no priorities (the schedule is empty).

Nan was trying to juggle two conflicting priorities: her coaching business and managing her rental property. Her calendar was a mess; because both her businesses were equally important to her, she didn't say no to anything, and she was often going from a coaching client session to handling her rental property without any time to change gears and present her best self. In working with my team, she figured out a schedule where she designated certain days and times for her coaching clients, while blocking off other times to work on her rental property. It was possible to prioritize both—as long as she kept firm boundaries around each of them so they wouldn't compete.

One of my favorite quotes from Jim Collins's book, *Good to Great*, is, "If you have more than three priorities, you don't have any."

What are your top three priorities right now? Is your business among them? If so, keep moving into the next chapters of this book. If not, spend a bit of time, like Nan, adjusting your schedule to reflect your priorities.

Going Pro Tip

Sarah, a driven professor, juggled a demanding full-time job, two kids under four, managing the household, and a burning desire to start her own business. Her often-competing responsibilities left her depleted and pushed her to exhaustion as she worked long hours, sacrificing sleep for the sake of her dream. Never having had her own business, she kept pushing forward, working on anything that would hopefully make her business work.

She was busy, but scattered and all over the place. She just kept pushing through. Eventually, the strain of it all became too much. The constant stress, lack of sleep, and unsustainable pace led to a point where, when we were having lunch one day, I was afraid she was going to face-plant in her soup. She realized that her relentless efforts had kept her sputtering on fumes and unable to be effective in any of the things she was trying to do. As a result, none of them went well.

It's important to set realistic expectations. The point is not to work long, grueling hours just for the sake of being busy. That's how martyr complexes are born. When defining what 100 percent commitment looks like for you, factor in your lifestyle, any existing job you may have, or other aspects of your life that will influence how you show up. From here, you can set clear priorities and solid commitment levels, and appropriate timeline expectations.

Sarah recognized the need for a drastic change. Acknowledging that her approach was unsustainable, she reevaluated her timeline for launching the business, understanding that success required a strategic approach. She learned to say no to certain opportunities, focusing on quality over quantity. When she established clear priorities and sought support from her partner, family, and friends, she could allocate her time efficiently. This shift in expectations of herself (and those around her) not only reduced her stress, but also allowed her to maintain a sustainable pace—one she enjoyed. She found herself better equipped to navigate all it took to be a successful entrepreneur, was able to leave her job, and could continue to take beautiful care of her family.

Going Pro Checklist

- Complete the Stair Step to Your *Why* statement.
- Write out what 100 percent commitment looks like to you.

PILLAR 1: EXPANDING COMMITMENT AND DEDICATION

- Share the "Always do your best" concept from don Miguel Ruiz's book *The Four Agreements* with at least three other people closest to you on this journey to deepen the promise to yourself to not confuse perfection with commitment.
- Identify your top three priorities.

Oracle Card Exercise
#30 Lightning

The forces of the upper world are investing their gathered energies to ignite you with a new inspiration and creativity. Allow this divine gift of awakening to take root in your being, and enjoy a renewed sense of clarity, passion, and vision.

Why is this the perfect message for you, right now, as it relates to this chapter?

Take a few moments of quiet reflection time to journal what the message means to you:

_____
_____
_____
_____

Favorite Frames

Take a moment to write down your top takeaways, key learnings, aha moments, and insights that stood out the most. By identifying these, you deepen your commitment to becoming a professional.

Here are some of my favorite frames to recap some of the key points in this chapter:

- Enthusiasm is not a commitment. Enthusiasm is a feeling. Commitment is what you actually do.
- Your commitment level lies outside of your comfort level.
- Commitment is different from perfection. "Always do your best"—*Your best today may look very different from your best yesterday, or tomorrow.*

Feel free to add your own favorite frames in the following space!

Pillar 2
DEFINING WORK ETHIC

> Success is liking yourself, liking what you do,
> and liking how you do it.
> —Maya Angelou

When I stopped dabbling in coaching as a hobby and made the decision to start my own coaching business, I was nervous. After being tied to a desk and set work hours for so long, it took a while to wrap my head around the freedom and flexibility of having my own business.

I went to my first coach, Kate, for advice. She told me that many coaches loved the freedom of working from home so much that they took it to the extreme. They would work in their sweatpants or pajamas while relaxing on the couch. Now, don't get me wrong, there's nothing wrong with that on occasion. But working in casual clothes can also mean approaching the work you're doing in a casual way.

Kate suggested, "Just because you'll be working from home doesn't mean you get to work in your bunny slippers. You will get dressed for work each day, just like when you had a job to commute to. When you feel professional, you'll act professional. That will make all the difference in how you see yourself and how others see and treat you."

I listened to Kate. Most every morning, I get dressed for work. I feel good before my day even starts. My dress code for working from home is not quite the same as in the offices I used to work in, but it's a level of professionalism that helps me exude a confidence my prospects and clients trust. Not to mention, I get to wear all the fun shoes in my closet.

The other tip that Kate shared with me was to create a workspace for myself. "It doesn't matter what or where it is. Just define it." She talked about the psychological importance of still "going to work" and "leaving work."

For many coaches, those lines between work and home get blurred. Our passion for coaching and our enthusiasm of wanting to help and serve others often leave us thinking, *I love this so much that it doesn't feel like work.* But if you're not mindful, you'll end up working all the time. It can quickly become a distraction and take you away from the other important things in your life.

Having a defined workspace will instantly create healthy boundaries for you and those in your household. When you "go to work" to your office space in your home, it's time for work. When you leave that space and "go home," now you're back in your personal life.

My first "office" was a sofa table in my living room. I had a laptop, a rolling file cabinet that tucked underneath the skinny table, my cell phone, and a lamp. That was it. It was right next to my sofa and TV. But it was my designated workspace.

PILLAR 2: DEFINING WORK ETHIC

After I got dressed for work, I would take my coffee and go sit at the sofa table to do whatever I needed to for work. When I wasn't working, I would leave that space. After doing this for the first several weeks, it became a pattern and habit. Even today, twenty-two years later, I still follow the same basic routine.

When the pandemic hit and my husband's company asked him to work from home, we set up his workspace at one end of the dining room table. That was his "office" for the next fourteen months. On one of his first days working from home, after we finished cleaning up the kitchen from dinner, he walked into the dining room to finish drafting a contract. I stopped him and asked, "If you were still working in your office downtown, would you get in your car right now, drive to that office, sit down, and work on that contract?"

He laughed and said, "No, of course not."

I smiled. "Then you don't get to do that from this dining room office either. Just because it's closer, easier, and more convenient doesn't mean you get to work at any time. If you're not careful, you'll always be working." After a quiet pause, he understood.

On the flip side, since the dining room was pretty visible from several rooms and a potential line of traffic through the house, we set good boundaries, like me knocking first so I wouldn't interrupt him when he was working. During our joint time working from home, my husband and I both took our work seriously, acted professionally, and avoided getting overwhelmed.

To navigate beyond amateur and embrace the professional approach, it's going to be important to stay true to your values, maintain balance, and find fulfillment in the journey without compromising personal well-being.

Thriving at the professional level is not a get-rich-quick, short sprint. It's a marathon. During my workshops, I'll often ask new coaches if they still want to be in business in two or three years. Of course, they reply with a resounding "*Yes!!!*" But sometimes they haven't thought through what it'll take to make that goal a reality.

To endure the long game successfully, it's crucial that your work ethic doesn't pave the way for overwhelm and burnout. Striking a balance is key.

Key Components of Defining Your Work Ethic

Let's explore important differences in how amateurs and professionals approach this pillar. Understanding these distinctions can significantly inform your growth in this area.

1. Time Management
   - *Amateurs* work when they feel inspired. They have less structured time management skills. They often work on their endeavors when it suits them or when they have spare time.
   - *Professionals* work consistently. They tend to be more disciplined in managing their time. They set clear schedules and prioritize their work to meet business demands and deadlines.

PILLAR 2: DEFINING WORK ETHIC

2. Workspace
   - *Amateurs* often work in informal settings, which can lead to distractions and difficulty maintaining focus.
   - *Professionals* typically have well-defined workspaces, equipped with necessary tools and free from unnecessary distractions.
3. Boundaries
   - *Amateurs* may struggle with maintaining a healthy work-life balance, especially if they work from home. The boundaries between work and personal life can blur, impacting their overall well-being.
   - *Professionals* are more likely to establish clear boundaries between work and personal life, such as setting office hours and dressing for success.
4. Risk Tolerance
   - *Amateurs* have a lower risk tolerance and may be hesitant to take significant financial or personal risks.
   - *Professionals* are willing to take calculated risks. They understand that entrepreneurship often involves financial and personal risks, and they make informed decisions to manage and mitigate those risks.

Work Ethic Does Not Equal Hard Work

If you associate work ethic only with working hard, you're missing perhaps the most impactful aspect. Yes, there's something to be said for hard work and getting things done. But by focusing solely on hard work, many take it to the extreme, working their fingers to the bones. Do any of these motivational quotes sound familiar?

> "Hard work pays off."
> —Ray Bradbury

> "There will be obstacles. There will be doubters. There will be mistakes. But with hard work, there are no limits."
> —Michael Phelps

> "I'm a great believer in luck, and I find the harder I work the more I have of it."
> —Thomas Jefferson

> "No matter how hard you work, someone else is working harder."
> —Elon Musk

These quotes, especially coming from such influential figures, drive us to work hard, then work harder, then still harder. But they're missing a crucial caveat: hard work needs to be in *balance* with enjoyment and rejuvenation.

PILLAR 2: DEFINING WORK ETHIC

In the early days of my coaching business, I was first and foremost supporting small-business owners as they turned their hobbies into businesses. They were working long hours, and rarely saw their families due to the constant demands. One thing they had in common was they all worked really, really hard in their businesses. They all adopted the belief, "If I just work hard enough now, eventually I'll be able to free up my time for what matters."

The if/then thinking kept them in a perpetual spiral of working harder, trying to outrace the demands. They ended up sacrificing what mattered to them and began to resent the passion they once loved. Through my coaching, they turned that around.

Still not convinced that hard work isn't the be-all and end-all? One of my colleagues, who recently passed away after a hard battle with cancer, had spent a lifetime focusing 100 percent of his energy and attention on working hard in his business. He'd built a very successful, multimillion-dollar coaching company, but his drive to succeed also led to constant travel, a divorce, and little time to live life to the fullest. On his deathbed, he said he'd finally realized that people who prioritized work-life balance had the right idea all along.

Hard work is closely related to work ethic and often one aspect of it, but there is a key difference: hard work is focused on effort and time. Work ethic is focused on the outcome.

Work ethic goes beyond the act of working, the actions you take, and the effort applied. It's also about how you set yourself up to take the necessary actions and work to achieve the desired outcomes.

Having a better understanding of work ethic, you can work smarter, not just harder. Combining committed effort with consistent action accelerates your success, even while still enjoying the other aspects of life that matter.

Back in 2016 when I first met Carol, she was recently divorced and a single mother of two, desperately looking for a way to generate income through her coaching business to support her family. She had been working long hours creating a lot of different income streams, hoping that at least one of them would make some money. The various endeavors pulled her in many directions. Her business was, as she described, "barely hanging on by spitballs and duct tape." We transformed her business and as a result, she is now able to have a thriving, profitable business while also being a thriving single mom taking care of her sons. She didn't have to sacrifice parenting for her business. Both priorities were possible because of her work ethic. In fact, when I was doing research for this book and asked for Carol's input, she shared this with me:

> I am beyond thrilled that I consider myself a professional. So much so that I don't even think about it. Maybe that's unconscious competence. And I have YOU, Melinda, to thank. Thank you for allowing me the opportunity to live up to my potential. I am living my dream. I am my own dream. And I inspire and empower others to do the same. And it just keeps getting better.
>
> —Carol Williams

When you take a holistic approach to work ethic, so much more is possible!

Leveraging Your Time

Many coaches work from home. It's one of the enticing aspects about having your own business. You can set your own hours and be as flexible as you like, which, for some coaches, swiftly mutates into setting no fixed hours at all. Because coaches love the work they do, they may barely think of it as work at all. While that's a blessing, it can also be a curse—your passion can take over and before you know it, you're working at all hours, at any place, at any time.

It's important to set your work hours, just as if you had a *j-o-b* outside the home. What time will you start? What time will you wrap up? Of course, your hours don't have to be set in stone, but they're there as a guideline for you and for those in your household.

Your Workspace Informs Your Workflow

The space you work in—be it a dining room table, a dedicated room, or a sofa table like my first desk—supports your daily activities and energy.

If you're working in a cluttered, disorganized space, then your energy and the quality of your work will also be cluttered and disorganized. Operating in this scattered energy makes it more likely you'll fall prey to the "shiny object syndrome" where you're chasing new ideas, trends, or fads rather than proactively staying focused on your goals. This state often forces you to work unnecessarily harder.

One of our students would grab her laptop and plop on the couch, or would sit at the kitchen table while her family was eating, doing homework, or watching TV. Initially she thought the ability to work whenever she wanted, from wherever she wanted, created the freedom and flexibility she wanted in her business. But the constant distractions from the noise made it difficult for her to get anything done. It wasn't until she claimed a dedicated work area (a small table in the corner of a bedroom in her New York apartment) that she was able to put concentrated attention on her business and make progress.

Take the time to create a workspace that is inspiring, a joy to be in, and supports the work you need to accomplish. It doesn't have to be fancy or elaborate, just clear, organized, and efficient.

Essential elements for any workspace include a dedicated surface space to fit your computer, gadgets, and accessories. It doesn't have to be a desk. The space just needs to be large enough for all your job-related items. Another important element is a comfortable desk chair, ideally not a dining room chair, as they're not designed to sit on for long periods of time, but that will suffice to get you started. And make sure to allocate some storage space to keep your business items and supplies organized. This could be a simple, rolling, single-drawer filing cabinet, a fixed multi-drawer lateral filing cabinet, or a bookcase

These three elements can easily establish your dedicated workspace whether you have an entire room for your home office, a converted closet of a guest room, an end of your dining room table, or a wall in your living room (all of which I've seen successfully support six-figure businesses). These elements help to establish your workspace boundaries and let others in your household know when you're at work and are not to be interrupted.

Other important factors to consider include high-speed internet with a strong Wi-Fi signal, a decent webcam, good lighting for professional video conferencing (be it a light ring, natural light from a window, or a lamp with the shade removed), a multipurpose printer/scanner, and a good headset or wireless earbuds.

Do Not Disturb: I'm on My Way to My Next $10K

The freedom to work from home can be a double-edged sword. The impact from the pandemic when many of us were working and schooling from home amplified the distractions. Pets were running and barking in the background during Zoom meetings; kids were asking parents questions in the middle of their Teams meetings. While it was necessary for everyone to do the best they could during the pandemic, having no boundaries led to never-ending distractions.

My friend and colleague Margaret Lynch Raniere has her coaching students create a sign to hang on their office door that says, "Do not disturb. I'm on my way to my next

$10K." This has a fun ring to it and is empowering to say, but it's also a nice reminder for her students and everyone in their household that they're doing something very important when they're working on their coaching business. It's a real business, and it's important to have focused, concentrated work time.

Maybe you want to create your own sign. Or maybe you just want to have conversations with your loved ones about when they should and shouldn't interrupt you during work hours. Either way, making sure you set clear boundaries—with yourself and your family members—will go a long way toward being productive and working smarter.

Mastering Decision-Making and Mitigating Risk

As a business owner, you will find yourself facing a multitude of decisions daily. Effective decision-making is a skill every entrepreneur needs. Without it, everything is going to feel both important and urgent. Surprisingly, though, even most MBA programs don't offer much instruction in the art of decision-making.

In a 2007 study, Cornell University revealed that entrepreneurs navigate approximately one thousand decisions each day. Some of the decisions you make in your business will seem minor and inconsequential. Others carry greater risks. Having a reliable tool to assess opportunities and associated impacts is key to making informed decisions and mitigating risks.

PILLAR 2: DEFINING WORK ETHIC

Going Pro Tip

To aid in the art of decision-making, I've developed a tool called the Clarity Quadrant. I always have my coaching clients complete this grid if they're struggling with a tough decision—and my husband and I have found it useful in our personal lives as well!

The Clarity Quadrant Exercise:
a decision-making tool to help mitigate risk.

Visit the Additional Resources section in the back of this book to download the Professional Coaching Business Tool Kit and a copy of this quadrant.

I always knew I wanted The Coaches Console to be a seven-figure business. For years, it hovered in the upper six figures no matter what I did. So I worked with my business partner at the time to locate a coach we believed could help us cross that threshold. He sent a proposal that outlined four strategies that would take us to the million-dollar level. He went into detail for each so we could implement them on our own if we wanted to. He even said in his proposal that he believed we could do it without his support.

He shared the investment we'd need if we wanted to hire him. It was a substantial amount of money, a lot more than we'd ever invested for a coach before. My knee-jerk reaction was, "We don't have that kind of money. There's no way we can afford this." I even went to our budget and bank accounts to see if there was any way I could find this kind of money. No luck.

I considered just taking his ideas and running with them like he suggested, but I knew the moment I had a question about one of the strategies or got hung up implementing the details from his ideas, I'd get stuck, and then I'd be right back where I started. I couldn't hire him. I couldn't not hire him. I couldn't decide.

So I grabbed the Clarity Quadrant and started completing each section. It confirmed the need to hire him. Using that tool and seeing the obvious next best step allowed me to get out of the "I can't afford it" mindset trap. It helped me shift my question to "How can I afford this?" I began asking additional questions, smarter questions such as "What will the return on our investment be?" and "When will we see a return on this investment?"

The moment I began asking those questions, hiring that coach was no longer a draining expense, but an investment that I knew we couldn't afford not to make. After determining the time frame of our return on this investment, we were able to work out an installment arrangement with him based on the added income we'd receive as we implemented each strategy. Within the year, after just implementing two of the four strategies, we crossed the million-dollar threshold. Shortly after that we hit $2 million. That coach was worth every penny that we didn't think we had.

When confronted with a decision that feels risky, take a moment to analyze the risks by writing your responses in each quadrant. Inevitably, one quadrant will have more answers written in it. That's often an indicator of your next best step. Being able to see all the responses of a completed decision matrix laid out in front of you makes it easier to assess and reduce risks and make educated decisions for moving forward.

Going Pro Checklist

- Establish your work hours.
- Hang a "Please do not disturb. I'm on my way to my next $10K" sign on your office door or in your working area.
- Set up your dedicated workspace so it's clutter-free and inspiring.
- Complete the Clarity Quadrant for any business decision, big or small.

Oracle Card Exercise
#6 The Blade

The blade represents sharpness of the mind, body, and spirit. . . .

The blade can be a healing tool or a weapon. . . . Use it wisely, and it will transmit power. . . . Use it with anger, and it will stab, slash, and kill.

You are invited to draw your blade and use it. It is not auspicious to hesitate, to waste time on idle talk, or to hide from the inevitable. Heaven and Earth are aligned to support you in claiming your power, so take decisive action. Overcome your fear of hurting others, unsheathe the blade, and use it wisely!

Why is this the perfect message for you, right now, as it relates to this chapter?

Take a few moments of quiet reflection time to journal what the message means to you:

_____

_____

_____

_____

Favorite Frames

Take a moment to write down your top takeaways, key learnings, aha moments, and insights that stood out the most. By identifying these, you deepen your commitment to becoming a professional.

Here are some of my favorite frames to recap some of the key points in this chapter:

PILLAR 2: DEFINING WORK ETHIC

- Work ethic does not equal hard work. Hard work is focused on effort and time. Work ethic is focused on the outcome.
- "Do Not Disturb. I'm on My Way to My Next $10K"—this is a nice reminder to everyone that working on my business is very important.
- Use the "Clarity Quadrant" to make well-informed decisions and get out of the "I can't" mindset trap.

Feel free to add your own favorite frames in the following space!

Pillar 3
CREATING YOUR UNIQUE VALUE PROPOSITION

> Don't be afraid to be different.
> Your unique value proposition is the magic
> that sets you apart from the ordinary.
> —Matshona Dhliwayo

One of my first coaching clients was a small financial planning firm with three partners. They hired me to help them reach their goal of bringing in the types of clients who would generate more revenue. But after I'd spent a few months coaching them, I recognized no matter what new ideas they came up with or how they tried to implement them, nothing was working.

They were not able to prepare for the client meetings properly or implement their new enrollment process. They could not streamline the way they were tracking data and give client portfolio updates. And behind-the-scenes obstacles prevented them from even reaching out to new high-value clients.

Now, general wisdom for their industry was to seek a higher volume of clients, rather than be selective and charge higher rates. This firm's plan went against that norm, but they knew it was possible, and I could tell they had both dedication and commitment to follow through. As a new coach, I was stuck trying to figure out how else to coach them to create their desired results.

Then it hit me. Thanks to my college degree in interior design and experience in corporate design and workflow efficiencies, I could see a problem with their office space. The people who needed to work together regularly were too far away from each other. The walk between the partners' offices took several minutes, and during that walk they would tend to get distracted by employees asking questions, leaving them forgetting what they meant to talk about with each other. They didn't have a great place to meet with clients. Even the type of furniture was working against them—the lack of ergonomics created more restlessness and less productivity. Until now, I'd been so busy following a standard coaching playbook that I'd forgotten to listen to my design instincts.

So, in one of our coaching sessions, I told them about my background in interior design and workplace efficiencies, and asked if I could present some ideas about how to redesign their offices and workspaces. They welcomed the idea.

I spent a few days helping them rearrange their offices and workspaces. Immediately, their team began to work seamlessly, and they were better able to serve their clients. By working in flow with their spaces, they were able to do more for their clients, which resulted in being able to raise their rates to be in alignment with the higher caliber of service—just like they'd wanted! Because they were making more revenue per client, they were able to work with fewer clients, freeing up more time to be with their families.

PILLAR 3: CREATING YOUR UNIQUE VALUE PROPOSITION

They'd hired me for my coaching, and by bringing my interior design and workplace efficiencies to the coaching relationship, I was able to help them achieve their lofty goals and get results quickly. What made me—as a coach—unique was the experience I brought to *supplement* my coaching skills.

What makes you stand out as a coach is more than just your coaching skills. To stand out and succeed, your business must deliver unique value and results, and you must convey a confidence that your prospects and clients can rely on in the midst of their own doubts.

Your Unique Value Proposition Is a Promise of Benefits to Be Delivered

Many coaches, especially newer ones just starting their business, experience quite a bit of doubt and uncertainty when it comes to talking with potential clients. They'll start letting the imposter syndrome take over, leaving them searching for any external factors that will help them feel more credible and confident in the early stages of starting their business.

One go-to "safe" move they'll often make is to get more certifications or take more classes. After all, learning is our comfort zone. We love to learn. So coaches will slip back into that mode, saying "*When* I get XYZ certification, *then* people will want to hire me."

The when/then thinking can be a dangerous downward spiral if you're not careful. While learning and certifications certainly have their place, sometimes coaches will hide behind them.

No matter how many certifications you have, they're not enough on their own to make you stand out. That's where your unique value proposition (UVP) comes in. Your UVP is the primary reason why someone should buy from *you*. There are various ways different marketing experts define UVP:

- A clear statement that explains the benefits of your product, how it solves customers' problems, why it is different from similar products, and why customers should buy it.
- An accurate representation of your business's capabilities.
- An offer that is so compelling that customers rush out to pay for your service.
- A powerful summary of who you are and what you offer. It defines what is distinct and valuable for your prospects and customers.

Key Components Creating Your Unique Value Proposition

Let's explore important differences in how amateurs and professionals approach this pillar. Understanding these distinctions can significantly inform your growth in this area.

PILLAR 3: CREATING YOUR UNIQUE VALUE PROPOSITION

1. Positioning
   - *Amateurs* will have a less informed, simpler value proposition.
   - *Professionals* are more likely to base their UVP on lived experience, market research, and strategic positioning.
2. Market Research
   - *Amateurs* often bypass market research, relying on their own assumptions about what potential clients value. Their UVP tends to be rooted in their own personal transformations. Often amateurs will resort to guesswork and use industry jargon to describe the value of their services.
   - *Professionals* understand the significance of conducting market research. They invest time in collecting the exact words and phrases used by their target market to describe challenges and desired outcomes so they know where the value lies for potential clients.

Your UVP Is an Important Tool to Stand Out in Today's Marketplace

Using everyday language to describe your UVP creates a stronger connection with potential clients, and helps you locate your confidence in the midst of your newness.

When you're beginning to think about your UVP, contemplate the following:

What style do you take in your coaching (are you direct, gentle, cheeky, etc.)?

Why do you matter? What are your beliefs/values?

What transformation does your business provide?

How do you help clients achieve that transformation?

What else do you bring that creates a unique experience for your clients?

What makes you stand apart from all the other coaches someone could hire?

I'll let you in on a little secret—it rarely has anything to do with more credentials behind your name. It also isn't about being vague and general. Once at a networking meeting, I heard someone stand up and say, "My perfect referral is anyone who is breathing, because I can help everyone." That does not help you to stand out.

When created, your UVP becomes a beacon for your business and marketing. It will inform what offers you create (or don't create) and how to clarify your niche, as well as helping make sure the imposter syndrome doesn't get the best of you. It will help you feel less skeptical about delivering on the promises of your coaching packages, programs, and services you offer.

Remember, this is not something set in stone. It's just what is true right now. As you, your business, the type of coaching you deliver, and the various people you're serving evolve, so too will your UVP.

PILLAR 3: CREATING YOUR UNIQUE VALUE PROPOSITION

How Coaches Get Their UVP Wrong

When creating their UVP, most coaches make it all about themselves—what is unique about them as a person, and their real-life, lived experiences that make them uniquely qualified to support their ideal clients on their journey of transformation. This is certainly part of what makes you stand out, but what matters most is the people you serve.

It's important when creating your UVP to use more of the word *you* and less *I* and *we*. It needs to be all about how you help *them*. In taking this approach, it will feel less like you're talking *at* potential clients and more like you're creating a conversation *with* them. You'll see some examples of UVPs in the following pages.

Make Sure Your UVP Is Easy to Remember and Easy to Repeat

Have you ever read a unique value proposition that a committee from a corporation created? Yeah, it's often filled with jargon and buzzwords. And as you're reading it, it sounds like Charlie Brown's schoolteacher: "Wah wah wah wah wah wah."

Instead, it should pass the café conversation test. Imagine you're sitting down for coffee with a friend and you're describing what you do and who you serve in a casual way. This is the same way you want to write your UVP.

When you share your UVP, you want the other person to remember it—especially if they're also interviewing other coaches. And you want them to be able to repeat it (or at least the gist of it) so they can easily tell others about you. Keep your UVP concise and focused, and avoid adding unnecessary or irrelevant information that dilutes your core message.

Beware: when trying to create something authentic and unique, coaches often end up identifying something that sounds good, but isn't a genuine reflection of themselves or their capabilities and might not even be what their clients are looking for. Your UVP needs to be authentic to you, so you should connect your statement only to services you can genuinely offer.

Professional Coaching Business UVP Examples

The following examples emphasize different areas of business focus:

- **Customized Action Plans:** "You will experience personalized coaching sessions with tailored action plans that are uniquely designed for your goals and needs, ensuring your success in every aspect of life."
- **Results-Driven Coaching:** "My proven coaching methods are focused on measurable results, helping you achieve your desired outcomes quickly and effectively, whether in your personal life or business."

PILLAR 3: CREATING YOUR UNIQUE VALUE PROPOSITION

- **Specialized Expertise:** "Our team of seasoned coaches brings extensive industry experience, offering specialized coaching in areas like executive leadership, career advancement, or personal growth, ensuring you receive expert guidance in your field."

- **Flexible Scheduling:** "I understand your busy life. My coaching services offer flexible scheduling options, including evenings and weekends, so you can access support when it's most convenient for you."

- **Continuous Support:** "My coaching doesn't end after sessions. I provide ongoing support through resources, tools, and check-ins to ensure your long-term success and personal growth."

- **Proven Track Record:** "My clients have achieved remarkable results, with testimonials and case studies showcasing their transformation and success."

- **Holistic Approach:** "I take a holistic approach to coaching, addressing not just one area of your life or business but your overall well-being. This comprehensive guidance ensures your balance, fulfillment, and success."

These UVPs can be used as a starting point to differentiate a professional coaching business and attract clients seeking tailored support and guidance in various aspects of their lives or careers. The specific UVP created should align with your strengths and the needs of your target audience.

UVP Fill-in-the-Blank Template to Get You Started

To get started, use this template. This may not be your final version, but it gives you an idea about what to include and how to articulate it.

> **Through my coaching services, I help you create** ___{insert result}___, ___{insert result}___, **and** ___{insert result}___. **Clients value my experience in** ___{insert something you bring to the customer experience}___, ___{insert one of the things you uniquely do with your clients}___, **and** ___{insert one of the ways you support clients that is different from what other coaches do}___.

You can see that the emphasis is placed first on the transformation you help your clients achieve. Then your UVP showcases the unique qualities about you that will help clients achieve their results. This will help you tailor your UVP to their specific pain points and desired outcomes, and show them how you can deliver value and an experience they can't get with another coach.

Here's a completed example:

> Through my coaching, I help you create a professional business that consistently gets clients and generates reliable revenue. Clients value my

experience in combining coaching with technology implementation so they're creating real results during the coaching experience. They find confidence knowing that I've helped thousands of coaches with their business. They also appreciate how I bring Spirit into business and cover not only tactics and strategies, but magic as well.

Now it's your turn.

Through my coaching services, I help you create _____, _____ and _____. Clients value my experience in _____, _____, and _____.

Turning Your UVP into an Effective Conversation

A big mistake coaches make when answering the question, "So, what do you do?" is to respond simply, "I'm a coach." That does nothing for your confidence, nor for the other person in the conversation. Their response is most likely going to be a polite smile and a "that sounds nice," rather than genuine interest and a desire to refer you toward your next client.

Instead, there's an easy format to talk about what you do so that people get it (and want to give you a referral). I call it your Five-Part Conversation, and it flows directly from your UVP.

I learned this simple template from one of my early coaches, Michael Port, from his book *Book Yourself Solid*.

When I applied this template into my messaging and conversations, people began to engage and respond.

> Part 1: What type of people do you love serving? (Keep it simple: just one or two words, max, that describe your ideal client. For me, it's "coaches.")
>
> Part 2: What are their most urgent challenges or frustrations that keep them up at night? (For my clients, it's "struggling to find clients and not making money.")
>
> Part 3: How do you package your services? (Again, keep it simple. Just "coaching" is perfect. Other simple examples would be "online course" or "group coaching program.")
>
> Part 4: If they could wave a magic wand, what results do they most want to create? (My clients want to "create a professional business making great money and doing what they love.")
>
> Part 5: What's your biggest success story (a client's or your own) you can use to demonstrate that your services have worked for others in similar situations?

Write down your answers to these five questions, plug them into this ready-made template, and your message is born!

Do you know __*{part 1}*__ who are struggling to __*{part 2}*__?
Through my __*{part 3}*__, I help __*{part 1}*__ to __*{part 4}*__.

PILLAR 3: CREATING YOUR UNIQUE VALUE PROPOSITION

In fact, __*{part 5}*__ .

So, do you know any struggling __*{part 1}*__ ?

Here's mine as an example:

Do you know coaches who are struggling to create a real business and are having a hard time finding clients?

Through my coaching and software, I help coaches to create a thriving business they feel confident about.

In fact, my client Ailish realized that what had been holding her back from starting her business was that, deep down, she didn't believe she could do it. Through my coaching program, and our work together, she realized she was hiding behind her fears and lack of belief in herself. She began to put herself out there in ways she never had before. She got the insight, clarity, and growth that comes from working outside her comfort zone. And she now has a professional business that she takes seriously. When we started, she had zero contacts, and she quickly added over one hundred people to her list, has enrolled a new client, and has secured two strategic referral partners to bring her more clients.

So, do you know any struggling coaches?

Practice your UVP and Five-Part Conversation message, and read your notes initially. Keep practicing until you don't need to check your notes to say the whole thing with confidence. Practice makes progress, which makes permanent!

Going Pro Tip

Know your audience.

Before you write your unique value proposition or create your Five-Part Conversation, understand who your ideal customers are, what challenges they're currently struggling with, and what outcomes they most want.

Alex, a life purpose coach who was just starting her business, struggled with talking about her work when people asked about it. Every attempt came off as generic. She was so uncomfortable she avoided social events where the question "What do you do?" might come up. During our discussions, it became clear she was reluctant to potentially exclude anyone, which pushed her into that generic way of speaking.

Before I took her through the UVP and Five-Part Conversation exercises, I had her first do a bit of market research where she gathered valuable insights from her target market. Almost immediately she saw common phrases they used to describe their challenges and desired outcomes.

Having this specific language made it easier to create her UVP and complete her Five-Part Conversation. Knowing she was using words and phrases that resonated with her target demographic, Alex felt confident to talk about her coaching business, knowing it would attract those she could help.

PILLAR 3: CREATING YOUR UNIQUE VALUE PROPOSITION

Use market research interviews or customer feedback surveys to gain insights into your audience's needs, wants, and preferences.

Market research can be simple. Reach out to three to five people who are either struggling in the area your coaching supports, or who once struggled in this area. These could be your past or existing clients, people you know, or people others introduce you to. While on the phone or videoconferencing, ask them these four questions:

1. What challenges [about your area of coaching] kept you up at night?
2. How did those challenges negatively impact your life?
3. What results do you most want [in the area of your coaching]?
4. When those results become a reality, how will that positively impact your life?

This will help you know what is most important to your clients and tailor your value proposition to show them how you can deliver value that they can't get elsewhere.

Going Pro Checklist

- Conduct market research interviews to gather the words and phrases your ideal client is using to describe their urgent needs and desired outcomes.

- Collect existing client feedback to better understand what clients most appreciate about working with you specifically.
- Create your Unique Value Proposition.
- Create your Five-Part Conversation.

Oracle Card Exercise
#12 The Coyote

The Coyote is the symbol of the sacred trickster, the one who provides detours for growth and understanding by ensuring that things don't go as planned. The Coyote brings the energy of divine deception to set you free from the shackles of that which doesn't serve you. . . . The lessons offered by Coyote may at first appear confusing, but they are most sacred and always for your highest good.

. . .Remember this: Coyote is a sacred trickster and may be leading you into challenges to ensure that you are ready to handle what you've set in motion. Great growth and understanding come to you when Coyote calls your name.

Why is this the perfect message for you, right now, as it relates to this chapter?

Take a few moments of quiet reflection time to journal what the message means to you:

PILLAR 3: CREATING YOUR UNIQUE VALUE PROPOSITION

_____
_____
_____
_____

Favorite Frames

Take a moment to write down your top takeaways, key learnings, aha moments, and insights that stood out the most. By identifying these, you deepen your commitment to becoming a professional.

Here are some of my favorite frames to recap some of the key points in this chapter:

- Your UVP should be easy to remember and easy for others to repeat.

- Having a simple template to answer "What do you do?" will help you feel more confident about engaging with others.

- Using four simple questions for easy market research gives significant insight in how to talk about what I do with confidence rather than guessing and hoping others get it.

Feel free to add your own favorite frames in the following space!

Pillar 4
ESTABLISHING ACCOUNTABILITY FOR OUTCOMES

> It is not your customer's job to remember you, it is your obligation and responsibility to make sure they don't have the chance to forget you.
> —Patricia Fripp

For seven years I had the fortune of being part of a business mastermind with Dog Agility World Champion and pre-eminent canine trainer Susan Garrett. She shared her philosophy with us about setting her dogs up for success while training them. When a dog she's training doesn't complete a command it's given, she does not start by blaming the dog. Instead, she first asks herself, "How did I fail to set up the environment for the dog to be successful?" She believes when the trainer can create the space and provide the tools to support the desired outcomes, the dog can easily win.

The same is true for working with coaching clients. (Not that I'm comparing people to dogs. The learning process just happens to be the same.) If you're coaching a client but haven't given thought to the space they're learning in or what additional tools would be helpful, then you're relying on clients to succeed while maintaining the very spaces and habits that have kept them stuck.

Support and Accountability Go Beyond the Coaching Conversation

A common mistake is that accountability is only about supporting a client to keep their commitment to a desired goal and checking in with them about their progress, offering encouragement and guidance to keep going when things get tough.

What's more, many coach training programs and several industry leaders reinforce this view, telling you the client is 100 percent accountable for getting results. However, I wholeheartedly disagree.

Hear me out. It's true that it's 100 percent the client's job to show up, do the work, and keep taking steps even when it gets messy and uncomfortable. But simultaneously, it's also 100 percent the coach's responsibility to create an environment conducive to success, offering the necessary support and providing additional resources to allow a client to "win," while smoothing out the friction points along the way.

During my days as an interior designer, companies would hire me because they recognized that they could have the best employees and the most amazing team, but in a poorly designed workspace, it would be extremely hard for them to be successful. While it was the employees' job to implement outcomes, it was the leader's job to make sure the employees had what they needed to succeed at the projects they'd been given. That included the work environment (hence my design work), job training, effective communication, up-to-date software, and more.

PILLAR 4: ESTABLISHING ACCOUNTABILITY FOR OUTCOMES

Susan always used to tell me, "Your dog is doing the best he can, with the education you've given him, in the environment you're asking him to perform in." Just tweak the wording to make it client-based and you have a maxim to live by. (Yes, I just compared people to dogs again.) Your client is doing the best they can, with the coaching you've given them, in the environment you've asked them to work in.

As a coach operating at a professional level, you are responsible for creating the environment your clients need to succeed. You share in the responsibility for their outcomes, and play a significant part in either facilitating their success or complicating their journey. It's your job to identify and eliminate friction points, ensuring a smoother experience. After all, you have the gift of experience and know the path that lies ahead for your clients.

Key Components for Establishing Accountability for Outcomes

Let's explore important differences in how amateurs and professionals approach this pillar. Understanding these distinctions can significantly inform your growth in this area.

1. Learning Environment
    - *Amateurs* just show up, are present for the conversation, and do the coaching. They think serving their clients is only about the coaching conversation. Beyond that, they believe it's up to the client to set themselves up for success.

- *Professionals* know that support and accountability go beyond the coaching conversation. The professional defines the space and tools a client needs in order for success to be inevitable.

2. Client Experience
   - *Amateurs* tend to prioritize their coaching without giving equal attention to the client experience. They may not be fully aware of the importance of a positive client experience in retaining and attracting clients.
   - *Professionals* prioritize the experience their clients will have, knowing it plays a pivotal role in achieving results and cultivating success stories. They understand their coaching is one aspect of the overall experience.

3. Client Success Path
   - *Amateurs* lack a well-defined success path for clients, often relying on the effectiveness of their coaching to facilitate breakthroughs and maintain client progress, even if it's sporadic.
   - *Professionals* chart out an overarching path to success, complete with specific milestones and clearly defined action items at each step. They understand the intrinsic value clients derive from this path, recognizing its role in achieving results.

PILLAR 4: ESTABLISHING ACCOUNTABILITY FOR OUTCOMES

4. Accountability Level
   - *Amateurs* often have fewer formal accountability mechanisms in place. They might not have established frameworks or tools for tracking progress consistently or thoroughly, which can make it challenging to measure client progress and outcomes.
   - *Professionals* establish formal agreements. They use contracts and terms of service, and set clear expectations for both parties. They have specific goal-setting frameworks, key performance indicators (KPIs), and metrics to measure progress (for themselves and their clients).

5. Tools and Resources
   - *Amateurs* may have limited resources to enhance the client experience. They may lack the tools, technology, or personnel to provide a comprehensive support system to the client. They'll typically rely on existing free tools even if the interaction between coach and client isn't secured or protected.
   - *Professionals* invest in tools and systems to organize and support their clients. They may use software, platforms, or dashboards to track client progress and communicate effectively with clients.

Accountability Begins with the Learning Environment You Create for the Client

In a world flooded with free information and filled with distractions, clients require greater levels of accountability to stay focused, get out of their own way, and achieve lasting results. Your accountability should be woven through your business's entire client experience, creating a client-focused approach to the coaching relationship.

This client-focused approach creates engagement beyond the coaching sessions, helping clients to feel seen, heard, and better supported. Better engagement leads to faster outcomes, more success stories, and steady referrals (ultimately making marketing, enrollment, and sales much easier for coaches).

By giving equal consideration to the entire client experience (or what many companies refer to as the "customer journey"), coaches will be able to stand out in an overcrowded market as the demand for coaching continues to grow.

Creating an Effective Learning Environment

As clients move out of their comfort zones to create change, they'll naturally start to resist (it's the natural human dynamic). The learning environment you provide for your clients should make their experience as smooth as possible while

PILLAR 4: ESTABLISHING ACCOUNTABILITY FOR OUTCOMES

they're navigating the uncomfortableness of change. Spend a few moments journaling about the following prompts. These insights will begin to reveal possible points of friction that may slow down or detour your clients.

When a prospect is first considering hiring you (or any coach), what are they thinking and how are they feeling in that moment of consideration?

_____

_____

When a prospect decides to hire you (or any coach), what are they thinking and how are they feeling in that moment of saying yes?

_____

_____

Once you have a new client, what initial thoughts and feelings do they experience one hour after they say yes? What about one day after they say yes?

_____

_____

As your new client begins coaching with you, what could prevent them from moving forward? What are some common elements that may cause a client to disconnect or disengage from coaching?

_____

_____

If you could wave a magic wand and create the optimal environment to make sure your client could succeed, what would you get rid of? What would you build in?

_____

_____

Often when I have coaches complete this exercise, they're able to pinpoint specific experiences or resources necessary to help their clients stay focused and make forward progress.

I was even able to apply this exercise to optimizing my own clients' learning environment. After completing several cohorts of our online course, I noticed a pattern that students were pausing or even disengaging from the course when they reached module two. As I investigated the situation, I discovered that the sticking point was a particular exercise that was an opportunity for significant breakthroughs. While the exercise was simple in structure, it brought up a lot of emotional struggles and limiting beliefs. When left on their

PILLAR 4: ESTABLISHING ACCOUNTABILITY FOR OUTCOMES

own to complete the work, many students would disconnect, disengage, or disappear.

To provide a smoother experience for our students and support their momentum, I added a private "Milestone Coaching Call" so each student could work with their assigned coach and be supported through the exercise. As a result, more students easily moved through the lesson, and experienced breakthroughs in their businesses. In fact, after her coaching call, one student said it was the first time she truly felt comfortable describing her work and that she was so excited she couldn't wait to express it to the world!

So, look again at your own responses to the journaling prompts. Your answers to question 5 will be vital to weave into the client experience. The insights from your answers will also be the building blocks for the unique experience you provide to your clients, so you stand out in an overcrowded market. You may not be able to build everything you envision into the client experience right away. It's okay to work up to it and build it over time.

Mapping Out a Path to Success Smooths the Client's Journey

When I was working with membership business expert Stu McLaren as my coach, he taught me the power of having a defined success path. In addition to defining the environment in which clients show up to experience coaching, professional coaches know that a well-defined Client Success Path offers numerous advantages, including clarity, self-motivation, and easy-to-track accountability. These benefits contribute to a more effective and satisfying coaching experience for clients.

Many coach training programs and industry leaders will tell you not to provide a defined path to success. They'll suggest that such guidance indicates you're taking a one-size-fits-all approach, and the essence of coaching is then lost. But a defined Client Success Path does not mean one-size-fits-all.

A one-size-fits-all approach is when you have every client navigate the same content, learnings, lessons, and exercises on the success path at the same pace with no regard to individual situations. This is indeed a bad idea, because your clients will have different lifestyles, different lived experiences, and different levels of comfort and risk.

However, mapping out a success path simply means pulling out any common denominators for the clients going on the journey of transformation with you—identifying the common steps, actions, stuck spots, resources, or exercises that *anyone* creating the same desired outcomes will need to experience or work though in order to reach the destination.

How each person navigates the success path will require your coaching, support, and accountability. The path is the same—the experience as they traverse the path is unique.

How to Create a Simple Success Path

1. **Identify three to five big, overarching steps.**
   These are the steps each client will need to take no

PILLAR 4: ESTABLISHING ACCOUNTABILITY FOR OUTCOMES

matter *how* they navigate those steps. This is from the 50,000-foot perspective.

2. **Identify one to two major milestones for each step.** For each step, identify the milestones so that, when that milestone is accomplished, the client (as well as the coach and everyone around them) will know they've completed and accomplished that step.

3. **List action items for each milestone.** Then for each milestone, identify a few key action items the client can take in order to accomplish that milestone.

4. **Include necessary tools and resources for the action items.** Finally, for each action item, identify the few critical tools the client needs so each action item is effortless to implement.

Here's my very first success path:

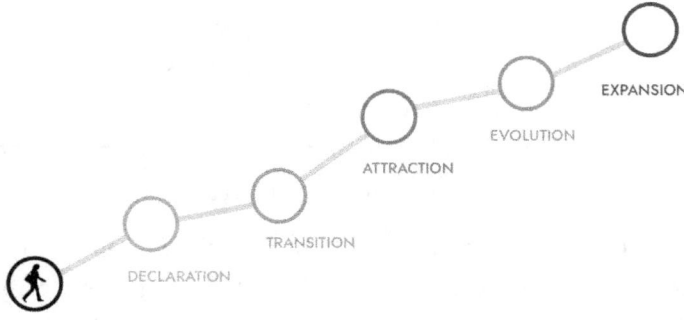

Example: The Coaches Console's first Client Success Path

The Declaration stage is when a coach makes the decision to start their own business. The Transition stage is when they move into list building (and maybe even move out of their job). The Attraction stage is when they start bringing in paying clients, and the Evolution stage is when they optimize their business for greater growth. Finally, the Expansion stage is when they scale their business and start building their team.

Breaking it down further, during the Attraction Phase, here are some milestones, action items, and tools that my clients needed in order to clearly know whether it was time to advance to the next phase on the success path or if there was still work to be done:

- Milestone: Add 100 contacts to mailing list
    - Action item: Create and implement lead magnet funnel
        - Tools: Simple software platform to integrate landing pages, opt-in forms, contact list, and online scheduler
- Milestone: Facilitate 5 sample sessions
    - Action item: Learn elements of effective enrollment conversations
        - Tools: 10-part enrollment conversation outline, online calendar

In a time when "bright, shiny objects" cause a lot of people to lose focus and get off track, having the clarity of the path's milestones and action items will help them to know where to focus their time and attention, and what

PILLAR 4: ESTABLISHING ACCOUNTABILITY FOR OUTCOMES

order to do things in so they're not skipping all around. This structure breeds freedom for your clients, not to mention faster progress.

I probably should have drawn the journey on the success path to look like this:

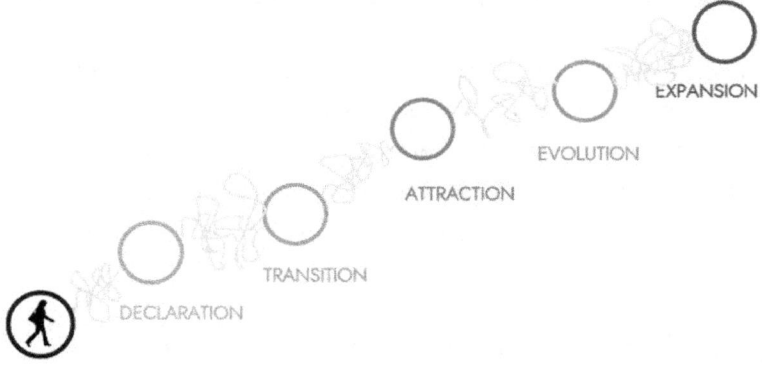

A more accurate representation of the client journey through the Success Path milestones

Your coaching, guidance, and accountability in the in-between times makes all the difference in the world. It's in between each of the milestones that your client's old patterns, limiting beliefs, and external influencers will get the best of them if they're not careful. How you coach each client in the in-between times is what creates a unique experience for each person as they make their way through the common journey.

There's a lot that has to be undone or unlearned in a client's life so that each milestone can become a reality. And that can get messy. That's why it's imperative that we provide a supportive environment and smooth out the friction points along the way. The client's journey is messy enough. We don't need to contribute to it.

Identify Areas of Friction and Formulate a Plan to Alleviate Them

As you work with more and more clients, you'll begin to see patterns in terms of where your clients tend to encounter friction within experiences that slows them down, causes stress, or takes more time than necessary. Two of the most common areas where coaches inadvertently create friction are communication and scheduling.

> *Communication.* Using email as a way to communicate important information, like session notes, recordings, and homework, with your client might be okay for a few initial messages, but keep in mind that email is not dependable or secure. Messages often end up in spam or get lost in the ether. And a client's confidentiality isn't protected as many people (family members, assistants, etc.) may have access to their inbox.
>
> Email communication often leaves clients wasting time searching through spam folders trying to locate something they need, or increases their stress as they worry who may read about private matters discussed with you. Instead, offer clients a secure place for them to send and receive messages from you.

PILLAR 4: ESTABLISHING ACCOUNTABILITY FOR OUTCOMES

Options include a texting tool like Signal with end-to-end encryption (messages can only be read or heard by intended recipients); a business messaging app for teams, like Slack, for confidential information sharing; or The Coaches Console, which provides your business with a private portal where clients can log in. The more secure and organized communication is with your clients, the easier it is for them to feel safe being vulnerable. And it's in vulnerability that great coaching opportunities arise, leading to breakthroughs and transformation.

Scheduling. While it may seem easy for you to simply email clients to schedule or reschedule appointments, the game of email tag creates stress and tension, not to mention added back-and-forth time just to pinpoint when to meet. Don't add to the stress of your client. Share a scheduling link for them to choose the best time for them from blocks of available time in your online calendar.

What are other areas where your client may experience friction when interacting with you that you can smooth out?

Define Accountability

At the beginning of the chapter, we established that accountability is more than just asking when a client will complete an action item or checking in on the progress of their homework.

It can be useful to institute a specific goal-setting framework such as the S.M.A.R.T. Goals Framework (Specific, Measurable, Achievable, Relevant, and Time-bound). This framework helps ensure that goals are well defined and achievable, and that they have a clear deadline. Another common framework is the B.H.A.G. Framework (Big Hairy Audacious Goal). This sparks creativity to think beyond known possibilities and dream big.

At The Coaches Console, we use a three-tier goal framework. For every campaign, we always set three goals: bottom-line, target, and mind-blowing goals. This helps us to know the minimum we needed to break even financially and keep our focus on our true target, while also leaving room to be wowed by even better results.

Key performance indicators (KPIs) can be another way for you and the client to measure progress. KPIs are measurable targets that indicate performance in terms of meeting goals. These insights will help provide quick accountability checkpoints to make sure client progress is on track (or if it's not on track, show you where to put your attention for quick course correction). KPIs will be unique to each niche and are important to establish up front with your client.

No matter what methods or tools you choose, accountability can be outlined within the formal agreement that you have clients sign at the start of the coaching relationship.

PILLAR 4: ESTABLISHING ACCOUNTABILITY FOR OUTCOMES

Establish Clear Expectations

During the enrollment conversation and even within your coaching agreement, you can clarify what coaching is and is not, what you expect of the client, and what the client can expect from you. Here are a few examples of the kind of expectations we guide our students to include in their coaching agreements:

As your coach, you can expect me to:

1. Be a partner in bringing out the best, the deepest, and the truest in you.
2. Provide safety, confidentiality, encouragement, and support in an environment in which you can relax and explore.
3. Press the edges of your comfort zone, expand your view of what is possible, and promote discovery of new insights.
4. Listen carefully to what you say, ask questions that increase awareness, and give straight feedback.

I expect that you, as my client, will:

1. Cultivate a core honesty with yourself and with me.
2. Be open to my feedback and keep me honestly informed as to what is and is not working for you.
3. Take ownership for your progress and your accomplishments.

4. Take financial responsibility for your coaching time. If you are unable to give a twenty-four-hour notice for a missed appointment, you may receive your coaching within the online portal.

Establishing these types of expectations up front, before they say yes to hiring you, can help train them how to be A+ clients. Your agreement can educate your clients about how to show up, what to do and not do, and how to make the most of their time with you for optimal results.

Invest in Tools and Systems to Organize and Support Clients

McKinsey & Company conducted a survey that reported the average knowledge worker spends about 2.5 hours per day, roughly 30 percent of the workday, searching for information they know they have but can't locate. Much of the time, they can't find the information as it's spread across emails, online chats, slide decks, documents, and spreadsheets. It's all disconnected and isolated.

Creating a secure portal, like what is built into The Coaches Console, for everything your client needs on the coaching journey helps clients reclaim those precious hours (not to mention how it will help lower their stress and increase their confidence).

PILLAR 4: ESTABLISHING ACCOUNTABILITY FOR OUTCOMES

Going Pro Tip

Many amateur coaches will ask their clients to create a folder in their inbox and save everything from the coaching collaboration there. Throughout the coaching agreement, the coach will then just email anything and everything to the client. While this organizes emails, it does not organize your client's total experience while they're working with you.

Professional coaches, on the other hand, provide client organization using a private client portal where clients can securely log in and access email messages, online appointments, forms to complete, payments to be made, and documents to download. This portal can also provide an easy place for any videos, assessments, content, or other tools you need to make available to them during the coaching process.

Let's say Joe reaches out to you at 6:45 p.m. on a Monday, worried about his interview on Tuesday. You recall talking to him about this earlier, and even emailing him a series of tips to help him prepare for the appointment. But you can't for the life of you find where you sent it to him. You're frantically scrolling through your inbox, after hours. Not being able to locate it, you miss dinner with your family, and quickly re-create what you know you've already sent. What if, instead, you had every resource you use with your clients organized alphabetically on one easy-to-access screen? You could just remind Joe to quickly log in and click a button to download what he needed, when he needed it.

Leverage integrated technology platforms, such as The Coaches Console, to organize and communicate effectively with clients.

Establishing accountability for client outcomes goes beyond coaching. You have a responsibility and a big part to play in helping your clients get results. The way you set up your client experience, the environment your clients will operate in, and your business will either contribute to your client's stress, anxiety, and overwhelm, or help create ease and flow as they make progress and create results. Which will you choose?

Going Pro Checklist

- Define the space and tools a client needs in order for success to be inevitable.
- Prioritize a client-focused approach.
- Map out your Client Success Path.
- Establish your formal coaching agreement or terms of service that includes specific goal-setting frameworks and other key performance indicators.
- Provide an organized, secure, private client portal.

Oracle Card Exercise
#32 Luminous Warrior

The Luminous Warrior . . . is impeccable in word and deed. He focuses on his light rather than on what hides in the dark. His power comes not from the sword but from speaking his truth at all costs.

Are you being tempted by your emotions to follow your lower instincts? Are you being invited to enter into a quarrel with someone? Put your sword away; this is not the time for battle. Do not act from a place of anger that will damage relationships. . . . Find the truth hiding in your heart that will affirm your instinct for peace rather than for war.

Why is this the perfect message for you, right now, as it relates to this chapter?

Take a few moments of quiet reflection time to journal what the message means to you:

_____
_____
_____
_____

Favorite Frames

Take a moment to write down your top takeaways, key learnings, aha moments, and insights that stood out the most. By identifying these, you deepen your commitment to becoming a professional.

Here are some of my favorite frames to recap some of the key points in this chapter:

- Borrowing the powerful question from dog training and applying it to coaching, you can ask yourself: "How did I fail to set up the environment for the client to be successful?"

- The learning environment a coach provides for clients should make the client's experience as smooth as possible while they navigate the uncomfortableness of change. The coach should not create more friction or make things harder than necessary.

- It's in between each Success Path milestone that the client's old patterns, limiting beliefs, and external influencers will get the best of them. How you coach each client in the in-between times creates lasting change.

Feel free to add your own favorite frames in the following space!

Pillar 5
DESIGNING DELIVERY OF CLIENT SUPPORT

> Quality service means exceeding your guests'
> expectations by paying attention to every detail
> of the delivery of your products and services.
> —The Disney Institute

Growing up as the daughter of a minister, I watched my parents successfully lead many youth groups over the years. Even in the small towns, with small congregations, it wasn't uncommon for my dad's youth groups to attract anywhere from twenty to fifty middle school and high school kids. Even kids from other churches would come join our youth groups.

One reason the groups were so popular was Dad's skill at planning adventures and trips for the kids. He'd arrange a weekend at an amusement park and water park, a camping trip to a state park, a weeklong canoe trip down the Current River in Missouri or the New River in Virginia, or a weekend ski trip in West Virginia.

In order for a kid to go on the trip, either their parents had to pay the way or the kid had to raise the funds themselves. Mom and Dad led a lot of fundraising activities—bike-a-thons, making custom sub sandwiches for Super

Bowl Sunday that we'd deliver to people's houses, or custom pizzas we'd sell, make, and deliver.

Many of the kids had never left our hometown before or ventured on a trip farther than maybe an hour's drive away. So getting the parents to agree was critical. Dad knew the parents were excited for their kids to have such a great experience, but they were also nervous.

So Dad took great care in deliberately planning every stop, every detail, every experience. He mapped out what campgrounds we'd stay at, and for multiday road trips he'd contact churches en route, asking permission for the kids to sleep on the floor for the night. He planned out meals, made lists of what the kids needed to bring (and not bring), and created forms so the parents had all the contact information to reach anyone at any time. Nothing about the experience was left to chance—to the best of his ability.

This provided the parents with all the necessary information, allowing them to feel confident about the kind of experience their child would be having. It also provided them with a sense of trust that Dad and other youth group leaders were cautious and careful when it came to watching over the kids. Dad made sure parents' fears were quieted and their excitement for their kids could come through.

Dad was always deliberate in communicating what the parents needed to know leading up to the trip, during the trip, and even after we got home. And I could tell he felt confident about being the leader. He knew he could organize and handle groups of twenty to fifty people and successfully, safely lead them to a great adventure that would forever impact their lives.

PILLAR 5: DESIGNING DELIVERY OF CLIENT SUPPORT

When I look back at all the time I spent watching and benefiting from my dad's meticulous support of his youth group kids and parents, I can see the foundation for the way I now support my coaching clients. I offer clear communication and set expectations before they even sign up for coaching and through every detail of their experience with me. Every time I get to watch my clients release their fears and embrace their possibilities, I know it's thanks to the way I structure my support.

So much time, effort, and attention is placed on getting the client and making the sale that the ongoing work of supporting clients often goes overlooked. Chances are, when you're doing your coaching, you're operating in your zone of genius, where the work feels effortless. That's a great feeling! But it can also make it easy for you to take client support for granted.

Remember, coaching your clients is one thing. Supporting them throughout the coaching journey is another.

When you intentionally design the delivery of your customer support, you can map out an experience that will help them feel confident about moving forward with you, create momentum quickly, and lead to even greater outcomes than they could have imagined for themselves.

Key Components to Designing Delivery of Client Support

Let's explore important differences in how amateurs and professionals approach this pillar. Understanding these distinctions can significantly inform your growth in this area.

1. Attention
   - *Amateurs* place their attention and emphasis on their own joy in the act of coaching. They love helping people and the rewards that come from regularly living their passion. It's mostly about themselves.
   - *Professionals* place their attention on the client. They are aware that providing high-level, extensive support contributes to a more positive client experience with faster and better outcomes. Their joy and passion for the act of coaching is secondary. It's all about the client.
2. Availability
   - *Amateurs* may not be readily available to clients outside of scheduled coaching sessions. They may have limited contact hours and response times.
   - *Professionals* build in various levels of accessibility into different packages and offers. They may offer additional ways to reach out between sessions in case of urgent needs (of course, this comes with clear boundaries and good time management, so the accessibility is not abused).
3. Communication
   - *Amateurs* may have inconsistent or sporadic communication with clients, which can result

PILLAR 5: DESIGNING DELIVERY OF CLIENT SUPPORT

in misunderstandings or dissatisfaction with the level of support.

- *Professionals* maintain proactive and regular communication with clients. They offer check-ins, progress reports, and structured feedback mechanisms to address client concerns and ensure satisfaction.

4. Onboarding
    - *Amateurs* are often singularly focused on getting paying clients, neglecting to establish a structured onboarding process. They jump straight to the first session or the start of the program and just begin coaching without taking the time to prepare or orient the new client.
    - *Professionals* recognize the critical role of bridging the gap between a new client's "Yes" and their first session or module. They leverage the opportunity within the initial minutes, hours, and days of enrolling a new client to establish organization and expectations, offer the client quick wins, and set a strong foundation for a successful coaching journey.

5. Processes
    - *Amateurs* lack well-defined processes and often handle tasks manually. They may rely on tools they're already familiar with, even if those tools aren't the most effective for the job. They make do with what they have.

- *Professionals* recognize the value of streamlined processes to enhance client support. They prioritize efficiency, aiming to provide clients with an optimal experience to achieve the best possible results.

6. Resources
   - *Amateurs* might offer basic resources and tools for client support, such as email or phone communication. They may not provide a comprehensive support system.
   - *Professionals* invest in a wide range of resources and tools to support their clients effectively. This can include dedicated client management software and/or a private client portal.

The Tale of Two Coaches

Let's look at two distinct approaches to supporting prospects and clients to really understand the impact on those you work with.

Meet Coach A: Fly by the Seat of My Pants Susan.

Coach Susan has been introduced to a potential client, Tom, who's interested in her coaching services. Susan has reached out to Tom to schedule a time for their conversation. In the email she

PILLAR 5: DESIGNING DELIVERY OF CLIENT SUPPORT

suggested a few days and times to meet, none of which work for Tom. He emails back to suggest some alternative times, none of which work for Susan. The email tag goes back and forth for about two days before they land on an appointment, which will happen in eight days. Susan emails her Zoom link in the final email and says, "I'm looking forward to our conversation."

Eight days go by, and Tom has not heard from Susan at all: no reminders, no additional emails. Just crickets.

Then it's the day of the appointment and Tom isn't sure if it was 10 a.m. his time or 10 a.m. Susan's time—and what time zone was Susan in, anyway? He scours through his inbox and trash folder trying to find Susan's email thread to see if there's any indication of appointment time details. He finds the thread but is frustrated as there's no mention of specifics. He anxiously emails Susan hoping to get an answer, but receives no reply.

Tom guesses that it was his own time zone and clicks on the Zoom link, hoping he's right. Only the message, "Waiting for the host to start the meeting," displays on the screen. After ten minutes of nothing, Tom assumes it must have been in Susan's time zone. He waits another hour, and clicks on the Zoom link again. Luckily, he guessed right. There's Susan. Finally. She asks him how she can support him and sits quietly, waiting for Tom to take the lead. Tom isn't sure where to begin and thinks, *Gosh, this has been so stressful and frustrating. Maybe working with a coach isn't for me after all.*

Meet Coach B: Professional Patty.

Coach Patty has also been introduced to the same potential client, Tom, who's interested in her coaching services. Patty reaches out to Tom via email letting him know about her excitement for their conversation. She includes a scheduling link for Tom to click and find a time convenient for him. In a matter of minutes, the appointment is scheduled to occur eight days later. An appointment confirmation is immediately sent to Tom, in his time zone, and he easily saves it to his calendar.

Twenty-four hours prior to their appointment time, Tom receives an email reminder from Patty. Included is a link for him to click and answer a few simple questions. Patty has explained the importance of providing that information so Tom can get the most from their conversation together. The next day, to Tom's delight, he receives another appointment reminder one hour before the appointment, including the time in his time zone so

PILLAR 5: DESIGNING DELIVERY OF CLIENT SUPPORT

there's no confusion, with the Zoom link also included. Tom is excited about the possibilities that will come from talking with Coach Patty.

Patty is early to the Zoom meeting, so when he clicks the link, she's there ready and waiting for him. She guides him through a great conversation, is prepared, and her attention is on learning about his challenges and goals. He feels well supported and is impressed, thinking, *If this is how she supports me before I'm even her client, I can only imagine the experience I'll have working with her. I think I'm going to like coaching.*

What did you notice about the differences between the two?

When I ask this question of participants in our workshops and events, they talk about how, in the first scenario, the potential client is left feeling anxious and frustrated. Tom has to do a lot of guessing and assuming; the coach has made it harder on him, leaving him more frustrated than when he started. Tom had to do a lot of the heavy lifting just to get to the appointment.

In the second scenario, however, the coach made it super easy and enjoyable for the potential client. Tom wasn't stressing about the logistics and details, so he could focus on what the meeting was meant to accomplish. The coach handled all the details so Tom could just show up.

Now, hear me out. It's not that the first scenario is bad. As an amateur, in the early stages of your business, you'll do the best you can, with what you have, from where you are.

In the early phases you may need to rely on email tag, for example, and that's okay for a short period.

When you have to use tools like email to go back and forth, it's still your responsibility as a coach to smooth that experience out as much as possible. It's important to be mindful of the stress or ease you're causing your prospects and clients.

But if you're an amateur for now, one way to act and feel more professional is to level up your communication, leaving email behind for a more streamlined approach.

When you spend too much time at the amateur level, without putting any attention on the prospect or client experience, you'll keep flying by the seat of your pants, hoping it all works out and you get a client. You'll have to reinvent the wheel each time, making it harder, not only on the prospect or client, but also on you.

Onboarding New Clients

In the previous chapter, we discussed the coach's responsibility to create a learning environment conducive to client success. This act of creating a good learning environment begins the moment a prospect says "Yes, I want you to be my coach."

It's common for newer coaches to send welcome packets to new clients, asking them to sign a coaching agreement, complete an intake or goals form, schedule their first session, or other basic steps necessary to kick off the coaching conversations to come. However, these are merely housekeeping activities. They're necessary, but a welcome packet alone

PILLAR 5: DESIGNING DELIVERY OF CLIENT SUPPORT

won't be enough to get your client completely oriented for the journey ahead.

It's helpful to leverage the enthusiasm and excitement a new client has when they first get started to build momentum and minimize buyer's remorse. That is done through onboarding—the experience a new client goes through to get set up and ready to make the most of their time with you.

A new client might be a little nervous, hoping they made the right decision to invest in coaching with you. The onboarding experience will help them feel like they've made a smart choice. It sets the tone for the coaching relationship and helps to build trust as the new client steps out of their comfort zone.

When completed effectively, onboarding:

- **Reduces client turnover.** Studies show that clients are more likely to disengage within the first thirty to ninety days than at any other time during a coaching journey. Onboarding helps build strong relationships and demonstrate value from day one.

- **Creates quick wins for clients.** The sooner your new client can experience small wins and generate momentum, the sooner they realize that change is possible and their investment in you is worth the cost.

- **Stimulates dopamine releases in the brain.** Dopamine is a feel-good chemical that reinforces the experience and strengthens connection to continue what they're doing.

- **Leads to more clients.** By delighting clients early on, you're far more likely to build strong relationships, be asked to provide additional services to existing clients, and gain referrals from raving fans.

Mapping Out Your Onboarding Experience

During a break from our mastermind meeting, Jason Friedman, a customer experience expert, and I were discussing how paying attention to the client experience makes it easier for clients to get quicker, better results. As he walked me through the key learnings he'd developed within his business, CXFormula, it quickly became obvious that within the first hour, the first day, and even the first week of a client signing up with you, there are golden opportunities to roll out the red carpet and set the client up for quick wins, helping them make the most of their decision to work with you.

Typically, when a new client purchases your coaching package online, it triggers a series of automated emails that start the onboarding process. The autoresponder series is designed to fill the gap of time between the moment they say yes and purchase your package and their first session with you. Here's how to onboard a new client in four simple steps:

Onboarding message #1: Congratulate them and validate their decision to move forward and create change.

Onboarding message #2: Provide access to necessary content or materials promised. It's in this

PILLAR 5: DESIGNING DELIVERY OF CLIENT SUPPORT

message where you'll also prompt them with an easy pre-work exercise to create a quick win.

Onboarding message #3: Share your Client Success Path and overall schedule (or access to your online calendar so they can book their coaching sessions). When clients are familiar with the defined path you've laid out, they can locate where they are in the process and understand how far they have to go. This clarity allows them to manage expectations, alleviate concerns, and take proactive steps toward a successful journey.

Onboarding message #4: Share social proof using client success stories. This inspires your new client to see what is possible, and becomes fuel encouraging them to take their next steps.

By implementing a well-crafted, automated onboarding process that bridges the gap before the first session, you're teaching someone how to be an exceptional client. This ensures they are maximizing their coaching experience and are primed and ready to create optimal results.

Exquisite Client Support

As coaches, we have the responsibility to put whatever resources we can behind supporting our clients so they have a great experience and get results. This level of professionalism is what turns your clients into raving fans who rehire you, refer you, and may even become strategic referral partners with you. So how do you implement exquisite client support? You design support for before, during, and after each session, as well as between sessions.

Support *before* the session:

- Your client receives a branded, time zone–specific, automated appointment reminder with the necessary details to make it easy to prepare and connect.
- Your client completes the Call Strategy Form included in the automated appointment reminder and submits it back to you twenty-four hours prior to the coaching session.
- You take time to review the answers and thoughts submitted on the Call Strategy Form before each session and prepare yourself to address those topics in the session.

Support *during* the session:

- You record the session, so your client doesn't have to scribble notes the whole time (and you don't have to remember what you said while you were in the zone).
- You store your private notes, thoughts, and observations from the session in a secure, confidential portal, which you can easily locate and reference to support the client in the future (and easily find everything when you need it).

PILLAR 5: DESIGNING DELIVERY OF CLIENT SUPPORT

Support *after* the session:

- Your automated system sends a Post-Session Recap Form to every client after every appointment.
- The client answers the simple questions on this form, to turn their aha moments from the session into actionable steps and new habits.
- You post the video or audio recording in a secured private client portal for your client to replay on demand.

Support *between* sessions:

- You give your clients access to a private portal where they can post questions, share celebrations, and upload homework or documents to be reviewed.
- Your client commits to using this private portal to reach out to you at any time if they feel stuck, whether it's the day after your latest session or the week before your next session.
- When your client indicates they need support between sessions, you send them a quick response with immediate feedback and coaching as well as a plan to address the issue in more depth at your next session if needed. This provides "just in time online coaching" to help your client maintain momentum and progress.

With this approach to support, your clients are fully empowered to make the most of every single day in their coaching package or your program.

A Common Client Support Misconception

Coaches often assume that offering support at this level will demand significant time and effort to implement and manage. There's also a misconception that this level of support is unnecessary until they acquire more clients—"*When I get more clients, then I'll implement more robust systems.*" That misconception is precisely what limits a new coach's growth.

Before joining The Coaches Console, one of our students manually onboarded each client by sending individual, custom emails with each new enrollment. In the beginning, when she was enrolling one or two clients here and there, it was easy enough. But as she grew and began enrolling more clients, she felt like she was reinventing the wheel each time. She also manually tracked and managed each private client, and with each new client she signed up it became harder and harder to manage them all.

She expressed her desire to work with more clients and launch a group program. However, she already felt maxed out in terms of her time, so she didn't see how she could handle more clients. She had put a cap on her own growth.

When we helped her implement exquisite client support into her practice, she was surprised by the outcome—it took less time to work with the same number of clients, allowing her to easily launch her group program. She is now making more money in less time, and is more effective as a coach to the additional clients in her program. Plus, she has

PILLAR 5: DESIGNING DELIVERY OF CLIENT SUPPORT

positioned herself to scale her business to whatever size she wants. This level of support not only streamlines back-end processes, but also adds significant value to clients.

Both the onboarding you establish and the support you provide will instill confidence in your ability to deliver what you promise and assist clients in achieving their goals. As a result, you'll stand out in a marketplace where potential clients are often interviewing multiple coaches before making a buying decision.

Support Client Organization Through an Online Portal

In my discussion of Pillar 4, Establishing Accountability for Outcomes, I discussed how professional coaches should provide an online private client portal where clients can securely log in and access everything, including communication, online appointments, forms to complete, documents to download, and assigned homework. This portal also makes an easy place to upload any videos, assessments, content, or other tools you need to make available to them during the coaching process.

Using an online portal, like the one included with The Coaches Console, makes exquisite client support simple and easy to integrate into your business. Creating a trusted place for everything your client needs on the coaching journey builds momentum, creating the opportunity for them to achieve results faster.

Going Pro Tip

The importance of offering your clients an organized, private online portal cannot be overstated. The same principle applies to you. Integrating a client tracking dashboard grants you instant access to necessary client information. When you can easily locate personal details you've noted about your client, upcoming appointment details, your notes from past appointments, and tasks and assignments they're working on, as well as other forms, materials, and content they have access to, you have everything you need within a few mouse clicks to track their progress. It not only saves you valuable time, but also empowers you to be the most effective coach for your clients.

For our twelve-week signature Coaching Business System program, we provide unlimited online coaching to ensure our students get the best results. In the first launch, ninety-eight people enrolled, and with only two coaches (my business partner and me), we were nervous about supporting that many students at once. However, our central online portal streamlined everything, allowing students to move at their own pace, access materials, and complete action items no matter what lesson they were working on.

At any point, we could pull up a specific student's dashboard and quickly review their completed materials, prior coaching notes, or other information that equipped us to provide great coaching tailored to their situation. Being organized made it manageable for us to handle nearly one hundred students without us being the bottleneck.

PILLAR 5: DESIGNING DELIVERY OF CLIENT SUPPORT

The second launch saw over 350 enrollments, but thanks to the portal, Kate and I efficiently handled the increased load. With plans to continue the program, we built a coach team who also used the portal to manage their assigned client load, making it easy to scale our program and business seamlessly.

When you're disorganized and struggle to find essential client details promptly, you risk wasting countless hours searching or, worse, limiting your ability to provide only mediocre coaching. A streamlined system ensures you can operate at your best professional capacity, meeting your clients' needs efficiently and effectively.

Leverage software, platforms, or dashboards, such as The Coaches Console, to track client progress and communicate effectively with clients.

Going Pro Checklist

- Create your onboarding messages.
- Establish exquisite client support in your practice.
- Organize your clients in a private client portal.
- Leverage a software platform to track, manage, and interact with your clients.

THE PROFESSIONAL COACH

Oracle Card Exercise
#42 The Rainmaker

The Rainmaker is the master of manifestation, who can call on the elements of nature to serve the greater good. When the power to co-create is used with integrity, great beauty and benefit flow to all. When this power is used for personal gain only, everyone suffers. . . .

The Rainmaker is calling you to create something new from the elements that are already in your life. Be sure you work with what is, and not with what might be or could have been. The seeds that have been silently germinating in your heart will burst forth ready for the sunlight. Do not hold back; put all your chips on the next roll of the divine dice!

Why is this the perfect message for you, right now, as it relates to this chapter?

Take a few moments of quiet reflection time to journal what the message means to you:

_____

_____

_____

_____

PILLAR 5: DESIGNING DELIVERY OF CLIENT SUPPORT

Favorite Frames

Take a moment to write down your top takeaways, key learnings, aha moments, and insights that stood out the most. By identifying these, you deepen your commitment to becoming a professional.

Here are some of my favorite frames to recap some of the key points in this chapter:

- Onboarding is different from housekeeping. Onboarding leverages the enthusiasm and excitement a new client has when they first get started to build momentum. It educates clients to make the most of their experience.
- Supporting clients goes beyond the coaching session, module, or lesson.
- Helping clients be organized through a central portal supports their momentum and helps them get better results faster.

Feel free to add your own favorite frames in the following space!

Pillar 6
SETTING PROFESSIONAL PRICING

> All underearners, without question, share one common trait: a high tolerance for low.
> —Barbara Huson (formerly Barbara Stanny)

> I have wonderful work, in a wonderful way.
> I give wonderful service, for wonderful pay.
> —Florence Scovel Shinn

Money doesn't grow on trees. Money is the root of all evil. We don't have enough. We've got to rob Peter to pay Paul. Growing up, these were the kinds of messages I received about money.

It's not that my parents were bad at parenting, or were intentionally creating thoughts of scarcity. Quite the opposite. I grew up in an extremely loving household. My parents were always telling my sister and me that we could be anything we wanted to be and do anything we set our minds to. But my father was a preacher, my mother a teacher; the reality was, we didn't have much money.

Why start this chapter about setting professional pricing by talking about limiting money beliefs? Because this is the number one factor that will hold you back from being rightfully rewarded for the transformative work you do in this world.

When it comes to setting your prices, there's both internal and external work to be done. If you only address the external (package or program prices, budgets, reports, etc.) without also addressing the internal (beliefs, patterns, habits), you'll remain in a constant state of tug-of-war against yourself—keeping you stuck as an underearner.

Money Beliefs Check-In

So, what are some of your money beliefs? Take a piece of paper and draw a vertical line down the middle. At the top of the left column, write "Current Money Beliefs." At the top of the right column, write "New Money Beliefs."

Place your hand on your heart and take a few deep breaths. Write down any and all current thoughts, beliefs, or feelings you have about money down the left column. Let it flow. Don't force anything. Your thoughts and beliefs could be negative and scarcity-based, or positive and supportive. Just write down everything.

Now, for each belief, thought, or feeling you've listed, ask yourself, *Does this belief still serve me?* If it does, then copy it straight across to the right-side column. If it doesn't serve you, ask yourself, *"What is a new version of this belief that would serve me?"* and write that straight across to the right-hand column.

PILLAR 6: SETTING PROFESSIONAL PRICING

Beliefs About Money	New Beliefs About Money
Money doesn't grow on trees	There are unlimited ways I can create money Money is an exchange of energy
Money is the root of all evil	Money can help facilitate good Money fuels my passion Money is a tool
We don't have enough	We are abundant

The Money Beliefs Exercise:
Make sure your beliefs are intentional and serve your current desires and goals.

As you navigated your way through growing up, you naturally picked up beliefs that, back then, seemed to make sense and serve you. The thing is, people often forget to check in with those beliefs to make sure they still make sense. Many people are essentially running on outdated beliefs that no longer align with what they truly want in life (or in business). It's only when you take the time to reassess and update your beliefs, thoughts, and feelings about money that you can start setting professional prices for the services you offer.

Key Components to Setting Professional Pricing

Let's explore important differences in how amateurs and professionals approach this pillar. Understanding these distinctions can significantly inform your growth in this area.

1. Pricing Mindset
   - *Amateurs* who recognize the importance of honing their skills and expertise understand the value of launching pilot programs or beta groups to build credibility, showcase their ability to deliver results, and gather valuable testimonials. They are aware in the early days that their initial pricing may be lower than their desired rates, but they view this as a short-term investment. However, when amateurs succumb to fears and become desperate to work with any client regardless of budget, they may find themselves adopting an underearner's mindset, which can hinder their long-term success.
   - *Professionals* firmly believe in the value they provide to their clients. They understand the need for fair compensation, considering factors like business expenses, taxes, and their own livelihood. They prioritize their financial well-being while ensuring that clients receive substantial value in return. They accept that it's okay to give great service and be richly rewarded for it.
2. Pricing Model
   - *Amateurs* often charge lower or inconsistent fees for their services—or even give coaching away for free. They may not have a clear pricing strategy, and may adjust their rates depending on who they're talking to. They often use simple pricing models that trade time for

money, without considering the broader value they offer. This can lead to undercharging for their expertise.

- *Professionals* establish structured and consistent pricing for their services. They often use value-based or result-based pricing, where their pricing is in alignment with the transformation clients can expect to achieve through their coaching services.

Sporadic Income Isn't Bad, It's Simply an Indicator; Keep Going

In the early stages of business, you're going to experience sporadic income—also known as "feast-or-famine" or "roller coaster revenue." It's natural and okay to feel a sense of sputtering when you first get started. Remember, in the early stages, you're still figuring out what you offer, how to package your services, and what prices make sense. So there's often a lot of inconsistency as you test the market and find your sweet spot. Be gentle with yourself while you're in this early learning and testing phase. Frequently evolving your prices is better than setting prices low and keeping them there; that's a recipe to keep underearning even as other aspects of your business grow more professional.

However, if you're an established coach with set prices (whatever they may be) yet find yourself falling short of the financial success you know is possible, it could be that you're letting your fears influence your pricing decisions. Try raising your prices. See what happens.

Keep in mind, too, that setting professional pricing is about more than just identifying a price tag for your coaching package, course, or program. It's about the additional skill sets, tools, and resources you include in your packages or programs. It's about the value of the results your clients achieve, and about the costs required to fulfill the packages.

Your packages and their pricing will be unique to the experience you create for your clients. This is yet another way to stand out in an overcrowded market of coaches!

Overcoming the Fears of Underearning and Embracing Sacred Success

Remember that story about me getting deep into debt in the early years of The Coaches Console? As I said, that was partly an issue of my commitment, that I was shying away from work I felt less confident about. But it was also an issue with my money beliefs.

One day, a few months after I started to make headway on my debts, I heard financial therapist and coach Barbara Huson speak about "overcoming underearning." Barbara related her own story of financial trouble, and described the traits of an underearner; that's when it hit me. I was an underearner. That's why my financial success was always so short-lived.

PILLAR 6: SETTING PROFESSIONAL PRICING

I dove into Barbara's book, *Overcoming Undearning*, took her workshop, and began to do the internal work of rethinking my relationship with money. In her book, Barbara defines underearning as "the inability to make more money despite your efforts or desire to do otherwise." In order to overcome my underearning, I had to embrace my relationship with money and transform it, rewiring old money thoughts, feelings, and beliefs. The more I dove into this work, the more my financial situation turned around.

Feeling encouraged, I read Barbara's next book, *Sacred Success*, which reminded me that it was possible and reasonable to follow my soul's path, for my own bliss and the benefit of others, while *also* being richly rewarded. And her earlier book, *Secrets of Six-Figure Women*, reminded me about the importance of having a strong Profit Motive (giving yourself permission to prosper without conflict or ambivalence). Armed with new, more constructive beliefs around money and now a confident Profit Motive, I was able to establish pricing that was aligned with the value I was delivering—without feeling guilty about it.

Amateurs can sometimes forget about making a profit for themselves, too swept up in the joy and excitement of pursuing their new passion of coaching. For them, it's not about the money. Amateurs have a comfort motive. But as Barbara taught me, one can never have a Profit Motive and a comfort motive at the same time. In order to have a profit motive, you have to value yourself and your services *more* than you value your comfort zone.

Time-Based Pricing versus Package-Based Pricing

When coaching first became an official profession and industry during the Information Age, it made sense to borrow a time-based model from other service-based occupations, like accountants, bookkeepers, and therapists. It made sense to charge per hour or per session for the information and insights coaching provided.

However, as the industry grew and with the birth of the experience age, it was no longer enough to just provide a great coaching conversation. Serving clients also had to include a great experience that enhanced the coaching. This was the birth of gamification, social media, and online communities as people got excited to be engaged in the learning process. So, while the time-based model still worked, it got harder and harder to justify prices based on time alone as coaches began bringing other skill sets and resources to give clients a great experience.

Some health coaches, who were also registered dietitians, included meal-planning services within their coaching packages. Career coaches included résumé-writing services and even helped facilitate job searches for their clients to ensure greater outcomes. Other coaches included retreats for accelerated momentum. Each of these examples supported clients in multiple ways beyond coaching skills to help them more easily reach their goals and end-results. Clients placed more emphasis on the experience, as opposed to just information imparted.

PILLAR 6: SETTING PROFESSIONAL PRICING

Now that coaching has gone mainstream and is no longer a nice-to-have luxury reserved only for the elite few, the everyday buyer doesn't have infinite disposable income to put toward something that doesn't yield results. We've moved beyond the Information Age, and the Experience Age is evolving. Today's buyer still values an engaging experience, but also demands that their investment yield concrete results. We've entered what I call the Results Revolution.

To appeal to results-oriented clients, you have to create packages conducive to client success, including whatever tools and resources you possess beyond coaching that will not only be fun and engaging, but also help them achieve results.

Beyond your coaching expertise, what other skill sets are you versed in that you can share with clients if needed? What resources have you collected over the years that can benefit your client's journey? How are you setting up your packages or programs to support your clients while they're working with you?

For example, drawing from my degree and experience as a workplace-efficiency interior designer, I support my clients in setting up their offices or team settings for optimal flow and better results. Drawing from my yoga teacher training, I bring yoga techniques to my clients when they're emotionally or physically blocked and coaching alone isn't enough to move them forward. Through my experience in breathwork and meditation, I help my clients connect to Spirit while they're pursuing their purpose.

Each of those elements has its own value. For example, interior designers typically charge $200–$1,000 for specific services like workplace-efficiency studies. The average cost to hire an interior designer for a full project is $5,400. The average cost for a yoga instructor offering private sessions is $60–$130 per session. When you hire a breathwork practitioner, sessions run anywhere from $30–$75 per session. All of these elements provide added value that I can integrate into my coaching packages—and charge accordingly.

Another example is my signature Coaching Business System program, where I take a hybrid approach to serving clients. Based on my years of experience, my clients are most successful when I offer a combination of online learning video content, group coaching, and private one-on-one coaching sessions, along with access to an online community, and technology for easy implementation of new strategies. There are a lot of costs associated with delivering that hybrid approach, including compensation for my team of coaches and the costs to provide the technology and tech support.

The pricing of your services must be a reflection of everything you bring to your clients, not based on outdated time-based models or driven by your own fears and doubts about money.

Misguided Pricing Advice

In just a moment, we're going to delve into the art of setting your professional pricing. However, before we proceed, a word of caution.

In our industry, the mantra "charge what you're worth" is everywhere. But beware! Do not succumb to this misguided advice. I've watched numerous coaches struggle with the challenge of establishing professional prices while wrestling with their perceived self-worth.

It's crucial to understand that *your* inherent worth has no correlation to the prices attached to your packages or programs. Let me repeat that (you may want to underline this too): *Your worth has nothing to do with the prices of your packages or programs.* You are priceless. No matter what you do or don't do in this world, your worth is priceless. Instead, charge what your *services* are worth in alignment with the transformation you provide! It might seem like a minor distinction, but it's the difference between remaining an underearner or doing what you love while being richly rewarded.

When you can feel confident about your packages and pricing and you believe in all the ways you're serving your clients, your enthusiasm and confidence will be contagious for your prospects. It will help them borrow your courage and confidence in the midst of their own fears and doubts to take that bold step forward toward the outcomes they most want.

Setting Your Prices: What the Industry Fails to Teach You

Most leaders teach you that, to set your prices, first determine the amount of money you need to make in a year to cover your lifestyle, then determine the number of hours you want to or can work. Then divide the first number by the second and it will tell you how much you need to charge per hour or how many clients you need to work with. Can you see the flaw in this approach? It actually keeps you trapped in the time/money prison. Instead, we're going to look at the Money Matrix.

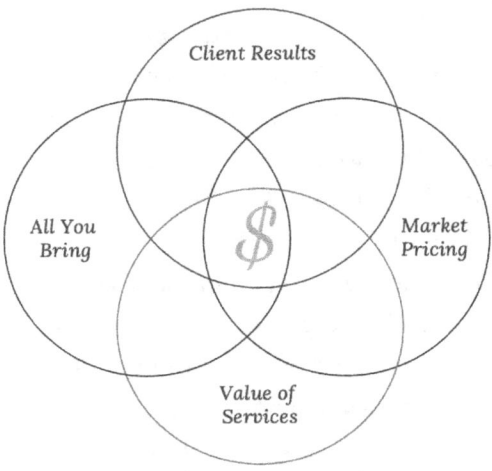

The Money Matrix: Four critical elements that influence the pricing of your services.

One of the questions coaches often ask me is, "Melinda, what should my package be? What's the average price for a coaching package?" If anyone ever gives you a blanket answer, pay attention! Coaching isn't a one-size-fits-all field. Remember, your pricing is based on the transformation and results people get when working with *you*.

There are actually four questions to answer to help determine your prices.

1. **List the results that are common for your clients to experience after working with you or going through your programs.** Assume they're an A+

PILLAR 6: SETTING PROFESSIONAL PRICING

client who will show up and do all the work needed to create optimal outcomes. Then give a monetary value to each result listed. For example, if a health coach helps their clients eat better, lower their stress, and improve their overall physical health, the monetary value would be the money saved from future doctor visits or from being able to stop taking certain medications.

2. **List everything you bring to your clients to support them in getting results** (coaching, prep forms, post-session resources, online private client portal, online in-between-session coaching, community, and other resources such as assessments, skills, modalities, frameworks, scripts, templates, technologies, etc.).

   Where possible, place a dollar amount next to each item to paint the picture of the true value you're providing. This helps you see the actual level of service you're providing to your clients, and will begin to minimize any fears of "not good enough" or "who am I."

3. **List all the reasons why your services are a necessity and not just a nice-to-have luxury.**

   To do that, answer this question with as many responses as possible: "If my client doesn't make this change, what are all the negative impacts on their life?"

   For example, regarding the work I do through The Coaches Console, if my clients—you!—don't make this change to become a professional coach confidently operating a thriving business, then you may have to get a day job or give up on your dreams. You may not coach anyone, and all those folks needing coaching could be left floundering, leaving the world in a funky place. I could keep going, but I think you get the idea.

4. **What pricing does the market warrant?** Not what do you think people will pay (in case your villains and gremlins are trying to run the show and price it too low). I'm not talking about your current comfort level. What are similar packages or programs going for in today's market?

   If someone doesn't sign up with you, what will they sign up for instead to get the same results? And what will they pay to get those results from somewhere else? Be sure you're looking at proven, vetted, successful programs to glean accurate market values.

   For example, will they hire a different coach who has a higher or lower rate? Will they join a program, an online course? What would that investment be?

PILLAR 6: SETTING PROFESSIONAL PRICING

Client Results	Everything I Bring to the Table	Why My Services Are a Necessity	Market Prices

The Money Matrix Exercise

Use this matrix to capture your answers to the previous questions. From there, you can begin to identify the sweet spot for your specific packages, programs, and offers. Your pricing should be in alignment with all you bring to the coaching relationship and with the transformation your clients experience.

You'll know you're in the right ballpark for your pricing if there's a little sensation of wanting to throw up when you think about saying the price of your package out loud to someone else. I'm not kidding. Barbara Huson shared this tip with me, and I'm passing it on to you. If you're thinking, *What?!?! There is no way I can set THAT price!* and you feel like you've got a huge lump in your throat and you're going to throw up a little bit—you're in the right vicinity.

Remember earlier when I described how it's normal to experience sporadic income in the early stages of setting up your business while you're still in the amateur phase? I'll remind you again. You're still in the figure-it-out mode, deciding what you offer, how to package your services, and what prices make sense. So there's often a lot of inconsistency as you test the market and find your sweet spot. Be gentle with yourself as you're in this discovery phase.

Two Packages to Get You Started

The pricing of private coaching packages, online courses, group programs, memberships, and masterminds are all priced differently. Your business model will also influence the prices you set. For this conversation, let's focus on pricing private coaching packages.

I want you to have a starting point for your research and testing. Start with two coaching packages. I say *two* because whenever you present options to a potential client, you create an engaging dialogue. If you just present one package, your client can only say yes or no. A negative bias is the natural human dynamic for most people. It's what I call "the knee-jerk no." They'll say no as self-protection, as a defense mechanism.

So it's wise to provide two options for your coaching package, with two payment options for each package. To get you going, borrow these starter result-based packages: the Jumpstart Coaching Package and the Total Results Coaching Package.

The Jumpstart Package is for the person who wants a quick jumpstart away from their current challenges and wants to begin heading in the direction of their desired outcomes. This package typically includes three sessions each month and

PILLAR 6: SETTING PROFESSIONAL PRICING

will span approximately three months (give or take). They may not experience everything they want to achieve, but they're going to get a few quick wins and some results. There's still more progress to be made, but they're okay with that.

Then there is the Total Results Package for total transformation. This package typically spans approximately six months (give or take) with three sessions each month. It's more investment, but it's ideal for the client who already knows they're 100 percent committed to the process.

Can you see how easy it is when you use result-based titles for your packages as an indicator of what your clients will experience? Potential clients can then easily identify if they resonate more with the jumpstart experience or the complete transformation.

Because you're now adopting a result-based approach to your packages, you'll set your pricing based on what you include in the packages to support your clients on their journey, not for the number of sessions within each package, and not for the number of months the package will span.

A good starting price point for your Jumpstart Package is $2,400 for the package. You can offer a 10 percent discount for those who like to pay in full. And you can also offer an installment option ($800/month for three months).

For your Total Results Package, a good starting price point is $4,800. Again, offer a savings for payment in full as well as an installment option that spans a bit longer time frame ($800/month for six months).

If you're reading this and thinking, "Melinda, I can't charge this for my packages," you're not alone. Many coaches get nervous because they've been underearners for so long and have become accustomed to low rates (even though they're not signing clients up at those lower rates)!

Just because it's uncomfortable doesn't mean it's wrong. Just because it's different doesn't mean it's wrong. It's new. It will take some getting used to. With practice, it will become second nature to describe your packages and share your pricing and payment options.

The flip side is also true. If your current packages are more than this, it doesn't mean you're overpricing. Go back to the Money Matrix exercise to confirm if the current prices you've set are in alignment with the transformation you're providing.

In today's market I continue to see all types of buyers still investing in themselves to create change in their lives. I can give you a lot of success stories for every niche, in every market. People aren't afraid to invest; they're just making smarter choices about *where* they invest their money and *who* they invest it with.

Adopting a result-based approach to your packages and pricing sends a clear signal to potential clients that you're ready to partner with them to achieve their results. It's about valuing the work you bring to the table and keeping the focus on them and their outcomes.

Having confidence in your pricing ensures that you are clear about what you're committed to delivering. It brings out the best in you, allowing you to be the professional coach your clients deserve, offering them the very best of what you have to offer. Your potential clients will pick up on that confidence, and it deepens the trust they have in hiring you.

PILLAR 6: SETTING PROFESSIONAL PRICING

Going Pro Tip

When one of our grads was first starting her coaching business, she was working in a full-time job trying to do coaching on the side. She was only charging $25 per session since she was trying to get anyone to sign up to work with her. Her fears and doubts had her believing that she couldn't charge much, since she was only working on her coaching business on the side and since she was brand-new at coaching. At $25 per session, though, she couldn't see how she'd ever be able to leave her job and go full-time with coaching.

We got to work on clarifying her business model, creating her packages, and setting her pricing. She launched six program cohorts earning $10,000 in group coaching revenue alone. She also converted group participants into her $6,000 private coaching package. That year she made $44,000 from coaching while still working her full-time job. Now she could start seeing how to replace her salary with coaching income. Shortly thereafter, she felt confident leaving her corporate job and pursued coaching full-time. The following year I received a text message from her: "Sending you my celebration brag as a way to honor the amazing work you bring into this world. I would likely be light years away from this milestone if it hadn't been for your coaching. . . . I had my first business say yes to my yearlong contract that will bring in $100,000. . . ."

Increasing her prices didn't cause fewer people to hire her. It resulted in the right people being ready to invest with her.

Let me share a little insight—I've witnessed industry leaders advising their students to just "add a zero" to their current pricing or pick an arbitrary high number as a strategy to boost their rates. I even heard one coach suggest creating a yearlong package and just charging $100,000 as a surefire way to make more money. The truth is, just hiking up prices without improving the quality of your packages or delivery won't magically enhance your services. It certainly won't help your clients achieve better results by magic either. The key is to charge what the outcomes are genuinely worth and hold yourself accountable for delivering those results.

On the flip side, it's essential to recognize that giving your services away for free or maintaining low prices out of fear doesn't necessarily translate to attracting more clients. In fact, this approach can inadvertently lead to low-quality coaching and a lack of professionalism. It's crucial to find a balance where your pricing aligns with the value you bring, ensuring a commitment to excellence in your coaching practice.

Going Pro Checklist

- Rewire outdated money beliefs.
- Complete the Money Matrix exercise.
- Prioritize your financial well-being while ensuring that your clients receive substantial value in return.
- Establish result-based pricing for two packages.

PILLAR 6: SETTING PROFESSIONAL PRICING

Oracle Card Exercise
#7 The Child

The Child knows the way to joy and happiness. The Child offers the return of a second innocence, a time born of wisdom and not of naivete. This card allows you to correct your course and offers you a second chance. . . .

The Child is here to release you from the habit of being yourself, and to help you acquire a beginner's mind so that you can see life as if for the first time. Remain open to learning and discovery. . . .

Why is this the perfect message for you, right now, as it relates to this chapter?

Take a few moments of quiet reflection time to journal what the message means to you:

_____

_____

_____

_____

Favorite Frames

Take a moment to write down your top takeaways, key learnings, aha moments, and insights that stood out the most. By identifying these, you deepen your commitment to becoming a professional.

Here are some of my favorite frames to recap some of the key points in this chapter:

- Doing the Money Beliefs exercise makes it easy to see why many coaches underprice their services.
- Your worth has nothing to do with the prices of your packages or programs. Charge what your *services* are worth in alignment with the transformation you provide!
- The four questions of the Money Matrix make it easier to determine pricing.

Feel free to add your own favorite frames in the following space!

Pillar 7
MANAGING BUSINESS FINANCES

> You can be financially successful
> without sacrificing your soul
> or compromising your values.
> —Barbara Huson

Robert Kiyosaki, author of *Rich Dad Poor Dad*, was a powerful influence on my life and money. Several friends, many of us all starting our own businesses at the same time, were reading his books and discussing them regularly. Kiyosaki also created a board game, Cashflow, which at the time was a big source of my financial education. The game went beyond understanding finances. It was a simple way for me to learn about creating wealth, investing, understanding stocks, business finances, and saving money.

Three of us decided to start "Cashflow Nights" as a way to get even more comfortable with money. The three of us would invite about twelve friends to a central location on the same night, where we'd set up our three Cashflow boards and split up the group for simultaneous gameplay. Afterward, together as a group, we'd talk about lessons learned and insights gained. It was a fun way to get comfortable with a topic I felt intimidated by. Playing those games and improving my financial literacy made it easier to handle business finances right from the beginning.

Understanding finances is an essential part of running a business. Many are intimidated by this topic, but it doesn't have to be as complicated as it seems. When I first started working with my bookkeeper and accountant, I would ask them to explain things to me as if I were a fourth grader. They agreed, using basic words that made it easier for me to understand and grasp the underlying concepts. The simplicity helped me feel more confident over time, and gave me a greater understanding of how my business's cash flow worked. It's important for you to prioritize understanding basic business finances, even if it's not your favorite task, to ensure the success and longevity of your business.

Key Components for Managing Business Finances

Let's explore important differences in how amateurs and professionals approach this pillar. Understanding these distinctions can significantly inform your growth in this area.

1. Level of Knowledge
    - *Amateurs* have limited understanding of accounting principles and may struggle with basic terms and concepts.
    - *Professionals* understand financial statements and typically have a higher level of

PILLAR 7: MANAGING BUSINESS FINANCES

    financial literacy, allowing for more informed decision-making.
2. Budgeting
   - *Amateurs* may have an informal budgeting and tracking strategy, making it challenging to track expenses and allocate resources effectively.
   - *Professionals* have well-defined budgets. They engage in financial planning based on forecasting future expenses and revenues.
3. Cash Flow Management
   - *Amateurs* often overlook cash flow reporting as part of their regular routine, leaving them struggling with unforeseen challenges when it comes to paying their bills.
   - *Professionals* place a strong emphasis on cash flow management. They use tools to regularly monitor their money, ensuring there's enough liquidity to cover operational needs.
4. Expert Support
   - *Amateurs* may hesitate to seek professional advice, relying on their own limited knowledge and experience.
   - *Professionals* are more likely to hire experts, like bookkeepers and tax accountants, to gain insights into the financial management of their business. This also allows the professional to free up their time and focus on revenue-generating activities.

The Wrong Question

What is the purpose of money in your business?

For that matter, what is the purpose of your business?

When asked, most coaches will share things like, "I want to help people" and "I can make an impact through my coaching." That's the purpose of your coaching. It's not the purpose of your business.

I'll ask again. What's the purpose of your business?

Your business is there as a mechanism to enable you to exchange value, make money, and create the kind of lifestyle you want to live. Money is the representation of the value exchanged. The financial metrics used in business are important to make sure your business is serving its primary purpose. Without the exchange of value and without money flowing through your business, it's just a hobby—an expensive one.

When I was interviewing Ann Wilson about the topic of professional financial management, she shared that most business owners start with the wrong question when setting money goals. Ann, a financial empowerment activist also known as The Wealth Chef, has been empowering others since 2012 to create their "unlimited life"—to do the things they love, experience a fuller life, and be safe and secure in the future. I had the privilege of being in a mastermind with her for several years. What I learned from her about money, wealth, and finances helped my husband and me to reach our own financial freedom.

Ann shared in our interview what the wrong question is: "How much revenue does my business need to make?"

PILLAR 7: MANAGING BUSINESS FINANCES

With this focus, a top-line revenue goal is set, often without consideration for bills, salary, and other expenses. Business owners often end up with nothing left to flow through their business to themselves.

The better question is, "How much *profit* does my business need to make?" By figuring out how much money the business will end up with once bills are paid, you're setting your sights on the right goal so that your business serves you rather than enslaves you.

Throughout this chapter we'll explore the necessary components so you can confidently answer the right question. That begins with unpacking basic terms and concepts to shore up your financial literacy.

Developing Financial Literacy

Amateurs do pay attention to revenue and expenses, but confusion begins when they try to look beyond the basics. To make sure we're all on the same page, here are straightforward definitions for some of the foundational financial concepts professionals need to be comfortable with:

Revenue	Income generated in your business.
Expenses	A cost or charge needed to buy, do, or create something.
Cost of Goods Sold	Expenses that occur to create a coaching package, program, or product.
Net Profit	Revenue minus expenses and taxes.
Balance Sheet	The tool used to track assets and liabilities at any given time.
Profit and Loss Statement	A report that lists revenue, expenses, and net profits for a specific period of time.
Budget	A spending plan based on anticipated income and expenses for a specific period.
Cash Flow Report	A list that tracks when money flows in and out.

When I first started learning about these terms, I was intimidated by them. Sure, I knew the terms *revenue*, *expenses*, and *budget*. The others? I had no need as an employee to know what they were. But as a business owner, I had to become comfortable understanding money, managing it, and talking about it.

The Lifeblood of Your Business

It certainly is a nice stroke to my ego to only look at the topline revenue amount coming into the business. But in the

PILLAR 7: MANAGING BUSINESS FINANCES

mastermind I was a part of, we had a saying: "It doesn't matter what you make, it matters what you keep." This mantra is right in line with Ann's advice to pay attention to the net profit, the amount left over after expenses. It's the profit that determines the true health of your business.

As my business surpassed the million-dollar threshold, we were able to maintain a pretty decent net profit while growing. I had colleagues who, while their businesses were making seven or even eight figures in top-line revenue, had almost the same amount of money going out of the business, leaving them with barely anything left over. Which business was healthier?

When you set an annual net profit target first, that allows you to work backward and better determine the amount of revenue your business needs to generate. If the income from your coaching business needs to cover 100 percent of your living and household expenses, how much money needs to flow out of your business to you to meet your personal needs? (If you have other sources of income that don't quite cover all your personal needs, income derived from your coaching business will need to make up the difference).

When I went through this exercise with one coach who is a single mother relying solely on her coaching business, after looking at her healthcare and insurance costs, as well as utilities, childcare, and all of her monthly expenses, she needed $76,000. If she was only focusing on top-line revenue, it would have been easy for her to mistakenly believe, "I need to make $76,000 from my coaching business." But that doesn't factor in her business expenses.

When you work backward, you can get a true sense of how much revenue your business needs to generate to cover all necessary expenses, including your salary.

Another client was retired, but loved coaching and didn't want to stop. She didn't *need* to make money from her coaching business, but she *wanted* to. She and her husband had plans to travel around the world in their retirement years. She wanted her coaching business to cover their yearly travel expenses. She knew she needed a net profit of $40,000/year to hit her goal. With that goal set, she was able to work backward and identify the amount of revenue her business needed to generate to reach that goal. Once she had clarity of her business expenses and the revenue needed, that better determined that her marketing didn't need to be very aggressive.

In the early months and years, it may feel impossible to reach your net profit target amount. But set your ideal net profit target, even if it feels out of reach, then work up to it in increments. Having a clear idea of the net profit destination you ultimately need to reach will help you prepare accordingly and make smart decisions along the way. It will also give you a realistic understanding of how you may need to supplement your income in the meantime (which I'll cover shortly) or how to adjust your marketing activities to generate more income. The clarity will help grow your confidence rather than fuel anxiety.

A Spend-Planning Tool

Early in our relationship, I told my now-husband about my financial debt situation. I had gotten myself $40K into debt

PILLAR 7: MANAGING BUSINESS FINANCES

and was in the early days of addressing it. At the same time, while he was an attorney, he had spent the previous twelve years helping his former in-laws as director of an outdoor wilderness adventure camp, making a modest salary. He had not saved anything for his kids' college fund (they were fourteen and sixteen when we married). We had a long way to go to turn our financial situation around, but we were committed to doing whatever was necessary to create a different reality. Thanks to the help of Dave Ramsey, author of *The Total Money Makeover*, we created a simple budget to track our money.

When the monthly budget was set, we posted it on the refrigerator so the kids could see it too. Whenever we or the kids wanted or needed something that wasn't already in the budget, we didn't say, "We can't afford that." Instead, we asked, "How can we afford it?" We'd look at what decisions needed to be made for it to be possible. Sometimes it wasn't, and we simply had to delay the purchase. Often, though, we could prioritize what was important and make conscious choices. Our budget became a tool of empowerment, helping us be smarter with our money.

The easiest tool to quickly gain financial clarity in your business is your budget. Most people avoid budgets like the plague. One of the common reasons is a fear that it will restrict their spending and they'll feel trapped. The reality is, it doesn't limit spending, it just redirects. Having a budget frees you up to make smarter, conscious choices for the things that really matter, rather than spending on what doesn't just for the sake of spending.

During my interview with Ann, she referred to the budget as a "spend-planning tool." That's exactly what it felt like for my husband and me—a tool that helped us get creative and make smarter choices in alignment with our life goals. Your spend-planning tool is about choice. You are the leader of your money. You get to choose where you're directing your money.

Another common reason people avoid budgeting is out of fear that they'll realize how broke they are. I grew up with "not enough" for a long time, and at times it felt pointless to even track money. The truth, however, is that more times than not, people find out they have a lot more than they realized. Without budgeting and tracking the data, most people have no idea where their money goes. It just "disappears." When you can be intentional about planning and tracking each dollar, you can make better choices, being purposeful about where and how your money is spent.

The key to successful budgeting is to let it be simple. Using a simple spreadsheet can be quite effective, even if you're making over six figures. Here are four tips for creating an effective business budget:

1. **Break revenue into categories.** Rather than lumping all your revenue together, track income based on the type of package, product, or program sold. By categorizing your income tracking, you'll see which offers are successful and which ones are not. You'll then be able to quickly assess whether you need to improve your marketing and conversion strategies for failing offers or put more attention on successful offers.

2. **Track fixed costs.** Fixed costs are expenses in your business that are constant regardless of revenue generated, such as your salary, internet, insurance, and rent. Tracking these can help set proper revenue goals.

3. **Track variable costs.** These are expenses that change in proportion to what is sold. When you sell more coaching programs, for example, there could be an increase in costs associated with the fulfillment of that offer. Some refer to this as "cost of goods sold." Other examples of variable costs include credit card merchant fees or paid social media ads. This helps you figure out when certain expenses may increase so you can plan accordingly.

4. **Track discretionary costs.** These are the nice-to-have costs. This could include things such as team perks, bonuses, and travel. Organizing these types of expenses together in your budget allows you to remember things you can easily adjust if necessary.

A simple spend-planning tool could look something like this:

BUSINESS BUDGET

	Jan	Feb	Mar	Apr
REVENUE				
INCOME				
Coaching Packages				
Group Program				
Online Course				
Membership				
High End Programs				
Retreats				
Masterminds				
Affiliate Commissions				
TOTAL INCOME	$0.00	$0.00	$0.00	$0.00
EXPENSES				
FIXED				
Rent				
Salary				
Taxes				
Tech Tools				
Vendor Costs/Employee Payroll				
Website Hosting				
TOTAL INCOME	$0.00	$0.00	$0.00	$0.00
VARIABLE				
Merchant Fees				
Sales/Affiliate Commissions				
Product Development				
Marketing				
Utilities				
TOTAL INCOME	$0.00	$0.00	$0.00	$0.00

PILLAR 7: MANAGING BUSINESS FINANCES

DISCRETIONARY				
Professional Development				
Team Perks				
Supplies				
Travel				
Bonuses				
TOTAL INCOME	$0.00	$0.00	$0.00	$0.00

TOTALS	Jan	Feb	Mar	Apr
Total Income	$0.00	$0.00	$0.00	$0.00
Total Expenses	$0.00	$0.00	$0.00	$0.00
Net Revenue	$0.00	$0.00	$0.00	$0.00

Business Budget Template

Visit the Additional Resources section in the back of this book to download the Professional Coaching Business Tool Kit and a copy of this budget template.

A Decision-Making Tool

Many amateurs will create and work with a budget when they're first starting out. But what they often overlook is the most powerful decision-making tool—the cash flow report.

Money will flow in and out of your business at different times. With your cash flow report, you'll see when income is coming in and when expenses are being paid. You'll know the exact amount of funds you have available at any given moment. This tool allows you to make smart decisions to keep your business healthy financially.

Every March, we at The Coaches Console have our annual signature program promotion. While we generate mid- to high six figures from that promotion alone, we won't see 50 percent of that income until the following month. The other 50 percent is then spread out three to twelve months after that. However, significant expenses are incurred in March, *before* revenue starts coming in. We use our cash flow report to help us estimate, well in advance, how much money will come in each month and how much money will need to be paid out and when. Understanding how our income is spread out for these program launches, combined with our expenses being front-loaded, helps us to plan accordingly so we can carry the added expenses and not get into financial trouble.

Your budget tracks monthly spending, but your cash flow report is most effective when tracked weekly. Because your cash flow report is a direct reflection of the cash currently in your business during a period of time, your cash flow tracking always begins with your current bank balance. Start with your bank balance, then for week 1 of the month, add in the income you're projected to receive within that first week. After that, subtract out the expenses that you know will be paid out in the first week of the month. You'll be left with a new balance to carry forward for week 2. You'll repeat the same process for each of the weeks within a given month.

PILLAR 7: MANAGING BUSINESS FINANCES

Here's an example:

WEEKLY CASH FLOW REPORT

	Week 1	Week 2	Week 3	Week 4
Bank Balance Carried Forward	$10,000.00	$13,810.00	$13,942.00	$11,245.00
Income - Coaching Package	$4,800.00	$2,400.00	$0.00	
Income - Group Program	$0.00	$2,982.00	$0.00	
Income - Online Course	$1,000.00	$1,000.00	$500.00	
Total Estimated Bank Balance	$15,800.00	$20,192.00	$14,422.00	$11,245.00
Marketing	$1,300.00			
Supplies	$150.00			
Internet	$65.00			
Travel	$475.00			
Payroll		$5,500.00		
Technology		$250.00		
Coach		$500.00		
Vendors			$3,000.00	
Cell Phone			$197.00	
Commissions				$650.00
Total Expenses	$1,990.00	$6,250.00	$3,197.00	$650.00
Estimated Ending Bank Balance	$13,810.00	$13,942.00	$11,245.00	$10,595.00

Cash Flow Report Template

Visit the Additional Resources section in the back of this book to download the Professional Coaching Business Tool Kit and a copy of this cash flow report template.

Our software programming team is located in Romania. We worked with them for years only meeting by Skype (yep, we've been working with this same team since 2008, before Zoom was a thing). A dream Kate and I had was to meet them in person. So, we decided to "meet in the middle" and book a villa in Italy. Having the cash flow report revealed the months we would have excess cash to set aside for the trip, while leaving enough to cover future expenses.

Using this report, we could see when we'd have enough money saved up so we could take the trip without going into debt. Each month, we allocated a certain amount of money toward our trip. Eight of us spent a week traveling through Tuscany. It strengthened our team and solidified our values of having fun while we work. We're still working with the same programming team and have since traveled to Greece and Dracula's castle, creating more amazing adventures together while doing work we all love—all using this same principle.

Understanding your money at this level can help analyze the amount of cash kept on hand to manage operational and day-to-day expenses in your business—making it easier to improve operations or increase marketing efforts (not to mention the fun).

Money Mondays

There's a quote from psychologist Carl Jung: "What you resist, persists." Deepak Chopra stated the opposite principle: "What you put your attention on grows." The more attention we can consistently give our money, the more it can grow, expand, and even transform.

Once you have created your budget and cash flow report, schedule a weekly meeting to review the data. Even if it's just a meeting with yourself, put it on the calendar and stick with it. Look at the numbers. Not only does this expand your comfort level with finances, but it also helps you understand how to interpret what the data is revealing to you. If you're not sure what the numbers mean, schedule a time to meet with a bookkeeper or accountant and they can walk you through the reports and translate the numbers. Even reviewing this with your coach can help you deepen your understanding and become more comfortable with money.

Kate and I would schedule weekly money meetings to review our business numbers together. It gave us each a chance to ask questions and get clarity. My husband and I did the same. Early on we established "Money Monday" meetings where we'd look at our finances. In the beginning, since I was in debt and he was living paycheck to paycheck, it took dedication to look for the small wins and stay focused on the bigger picture. Over time, though, the numbers changed, the debt went down, and the income grew. While we don't meet weekly anymore, we still meet consistently to put attention on our money and make sure it continues to grow.

Hurting the Credibility of Your Business

A common mistake amateurs make is to have only one bank account for both their personal finances and business finances. Especially in the beginning, when not a lot of money is coming in yet and there are minimal expenses, it can be easy to fall into the trap of having everything all together. Many new coaches I talk to will say things like, "It's just quicker and easier, because the money I'm getting from my coaching needs to pay my bills, which are due right now."

While it might be quicker in that moment, you're setting yourself up to have poor visibility into the true financial picture of your business. This can make it difficult to track business expenses and income, lead to a false sense of profitability (or exaggerated sense of expenses), and can lead to tax issues that could be hard to clear up. If you're using personal money to cover costs, it can deplete your savings quicker than you realize, damaging your personal finances.

Commingling funds can also hurt your business's credibility. If you mix personal and business finances, it can make your business look unprofessional and unorganized. Even if you're not making much money yet, prepare for and plan for the future. Set up a separate bank account for your business and have a debit card specifically for business expenses. Build the habit early, so it's easy to grow and scale in the future.

The Power of a Bridge Job

You might be thinking, *Melinda, that sounds nice, but I'm just getting started and I'm not making any money yet. There's nothing to track.* I get it. Even from day one, it's important to educate yourself on these terms, concepts, and strategies so when you do start making money, you're engaging in professional money management right from the start. It does a lot for your confidence. That added confidence will help you feel better about all money conversations—enrollment calls, sales presentations, and meetings with your spouse or accountant.

When I first started my coaching business, I was recently divorced and on my own for the first time in my life. I still had savings from my corporate job to carry me a few months. But

PILLAR 7: MANAGING BUSINESS FINANCES

I had to make money fast. I was able to generate more than enough income from coaching within several months to more than cover my business and personal expenses. But I know not all coaches have that experience. For many coaches, they need to keep their full-time job or get a bridge job.

A bridge job can be a fantastic solution to help bridge the gap in income and minimize anxiety when making the transition to start your own business. Trying to get started from a place of desperation can make the journey even harder. There's no shame in getting a bridge job. Quite the opposite. When you have financial stability from a bridge job, that helps with emotional stability as well. You can think more clearly, see opportunities easier, and make better decisions for your business (and life). That healthier energy will go a long way when you're navigating the uncharted territory of your new business.

A bridge job is temporary. It's designed to take minimal effort; when you leave at the end of the day, you don't take it with you. It's not a career, and doesn't even have to be related to your prior career or new business. Often for an amateur, it can be a smart business decision to leave a job or career that is "sucking the life out of you" and get a bridge job as you begin your coaching business.

If you have a good (or okay) career, it's okay to shift your paradigm and start seeing that existing job as your bridge job. Doing so can help cut energetic and emotional ties to something you once may have felt a lot of passion for. It can make it easier to walk away when the time comes, and head toward the new endeavor you're starting.

Professional Support

In the early years of your business, it can be enough to rely on your own knowledge and ability to track and manage your business finances. In fact, when you're the one managing your finances in the beginning, it can help you learn what you need to know and understand how money works in your business. For an amateur, growing this competence with your business finances goes a long way to increasing your confidence overall. At some point, however, it will be time to hire expert support from bookkeepers, accountants, and tax planners (unless, of course, that is your zone of genius).

To start, it was my and (my business partner) Kate's name on every spot of our organizational chart for the first year of our business. I was the one handling the bookkeeping and reporting. I was pretty good at managing money (keep in mind, this is before I got into money trouble), but it still took me a long time as it was not my strong suit. Just one report took me all day to create, update, and finalize. We made do with what we had, and it worked in the beginning.

It wasn't too long before I felt the pressure of the time spent working in QuickBooks and how it was preventing me from spending time getting clients. I knew we needed a bookkeeper, but we didn't have enough money to hire one. But we weren't making much money because I was spending my time doing the money management. Something had to give. We found Ruth, a part-time bookkeeper, and knew she would be a great fit.

PILLAR 7: MANAGING BUSINESS FINANCES

When I learned that her hourly rate was $20, I told Kate, "There's no way we can afford her!" Having never hired anyone, the mistake I made was taking her hourly rate and multiplying it by the number of hours it was taking *me* to do all the bookkeeping tasks. What took me an entire day, took her twenty minutes. Not to mention, she did it far better! Once I realized and corrected my ridiculous thinking, I was able to get an accurate idea of how much she would cost the business.

I calculated the time I would recoup and could spend on networking and revenue-generating activities, and was able to project how much more revenue the business would make by me letting go of this role. We could clearly see when we'd make the return on our investment of hiring Ruth. A mistake amateurs often make is to only look at costs as an expense. Failing to look at the return on that expense can prevent smart decisions from happening. When you can calculate what your return should be and when you'll recoup the investment, you can move forward with opportunities you otherwise would have overlooked.

A bookkeeper is often one of the first hires a coach will make in their business. A close second is a virtual assistant to help with various admin tasks. Both of these roles free up your time to focus on getting and serving clients.

Enlisting the services of an accountant enables you to save time and have better accuracy with your finances. Where bookkeepers focus on data entry and reporting, accountants help create budgets, provide tax-planning, and develop long-term financial strategies for growth.

At the amateur level, many *hope* they won't owe any taxes come year-end. The uncertainty of it and lack of planning contributes to higher stress and anxiety. Professionals, though, look ahead and plan for taxes. They're working with accountants to utilize their business to minimize their tax liabilities.

Many of my colleagues hold the philosophy to keep as much of their money in their hands as possible, for as long as possible. As a result, they don't pay estimated taxes (I don't recommend this). They prefer to make use of their money immediately, and are willing to write a large tax check each year. I, on the other hand, never want to be surprised when tax time comes. I don't want to find out that all of a sudden we owe a huge amount in taxes—maybe more than we have to spare.

As a result, I meet with our accountant quarterly and do mock tax plans based on our actual year-to-date finances and our budgeted finances for the remainder of the year. Having this regular meeting helps my accountant to better understand my business. He is in a position to help me know what personal expenses should actually be run through the business (because they were in fact business expenses). And he helps me minimize our taxable income and adjust our estimated payments so we could be as close to breakeven as possible and minimize tax risks.

The great thing about both bookkeepers and accountants is that you can work with them on a part-time, as-needed basis. When you utilize their services, you can free up your time and increase your confidence, both of which can boost your income and bottom line.

PILLAR 7: MANAGING BUSINESS FINANCES

Leveraging Your Money for Good

As I mentioned at the beginning of the chapter, the purpose of your business is for money to flow through it to you. You get to choose how you direct your money—does it cover your personal finances? Does it support a favorite cause? Do you use it to support your kids? A dream vacation?

There's a plaque my mom gave me that sits on my office bookshelf; it says, "It's a rare person who can take care of hearts while also taking care of business." Whenever I see it, it makes me feel good knowing I'm accomplishing both at the same time. I'm taking care of our clients, and I'm taking care of our team. And I know we can still do more.

As soon as I knew the business was consistently spending less than we were earning, saving a portion of our revenue, and investing it wisely, I knew it was time to start giving generously. So we created our "Taking Care of Hearts" give-back campaign. Through that program we've given portions of our launch proceeds to charity organizations, and we've instituted a "Pay What You Can" model for our live events in which all ticket proceeds go to a charitable cause. Over the years, we've contributed tens of thousands of dollars to various endeavors.

It was several years into our business before we could give in this way, but it was worth the wait. You may not be able to leverage your money in this manner right out of the gate, but having it as a future goal can be a source of inspiration.

Cultivating financial literacy, leveraging comprehensive financial reporting, and seeking professional advice are not just best practices of a professional; they are essential elements that contribute to the resilience and sustained growth of any business. The earlier you can begin to learn and become familiar with the fundamentals shared in this chapter, the more confident and successful you'll be as you help your business realize its full potential.

Going Pro Tip

Get smart with money from day one when you don't have much revenue coming in or expenses going out. The sooner you can establish professional practices, even when it doesn't feel necessary, the better you'll set yourself up for money management and decision-making in the future when the numbers get bigger and more complex.

One of the smartest things you can do early on is to pay yourself. It can be tempting to put everything into your business. Some even believe it's selfish to take money from their business. But not paying yourself can harbor resentment and even lead to burnout.

It's important not to overlook your role in the business, and to pay yourself accordingly. Paying yourself can actually be one of the most *selfless* things you can do. After all, it ensures your needs are met so you're able to show up fully as your best self—intellectually, emotionally, physically, and energetically—and bring all your resources to building your business. Being fully resourced also helps you show up as the best coach you can be. This kick-starts the flywheel of clients getting results and offering testimonials and rave reviews, leading to more referrals, making it easier to get clients, and generating more revenue in your business.

Going Pro Checklist

- Increase your financial literacy by getting familiar and comfortable with the terms and concepts in business. Whether it's reading a book, playing the Cashflow board game, or talking with a colleague about this topic, do something every week that expands your knowledge.
- Open a business bank account.
- Pay yourself.
- Create a simple budget.
- Create your cash flow report.
- Schedule a weekly meeting to review the numbers in your business.
- Identify a cause you would love to support when your profitability reaches a certain point.

Oracle Card Exercise
#11 The Council

The Council are the luminous beings who hold the collective wisdom of humanity. They are the ones before whom you will do your life review when you cross into the world of Spirit. Know that their wisdom is available to you at all times when you live in the state of yes, in an unconditional relationship with life. They remind you of your place around the sacred fire, which has been reserved for you since the beginning of time. You will claim it when you own your inner wisdom.

You are never alone. Turn to the Council to find the guidance you seek, and listen to the voice that arises spontaneously. Turn a deaf ear to that nagging voice from your ego that tells you that you are not up for the task before you. Create a spiritual feast for the Council; invite them to your altar every time you meditate or pray.

Why is this the perfect message for you, right now, as it relates to this chapter?

Take a few moments of quiet reflection time to journal what the message means to you:

_____

_____

_____

_____

Favorite Frames

Take a moment to write down your top takeaways, key learnings, aha moments, and insights that stood out the most. By identifying these, you deepen your commitment to becoming a professional.

PILLAR 7: MANAGING BUSINESS FINANCES

Here are some of my favorite frames to recap some of the key points in this chapter:

- The purpose of your business: to be a mechanism to exchange value, make money, and create the kind of lifestyle you want to live; money is the representation of the value exchanged.
- Set an annual net profit target first, then work backward and determine the revenue your business needs to generate.
- Money Monday meetings: The more attention you can consistently give your money, the more it can grow, expand, and even transform.

Feel free to add your own favorite frames in the following space!

Pillar 8
IMPLEMENTING BUSINESS OPERATIONS

> If your business depends on you,
> you don't own a business—you have a job.
> —Michael E. Gerber

> Spend time upfront to invest in systems and
> processes to make long-term growth sustainable.
> —Jeff Platt

Interior design was more to me than just a college degree and a fun career. When I was eleven and twelve years old, I'd close myself in my bedroom and rearrange my furniture. By thirteen, I knew I wanted to go to college to be an interior designer. I ended up in corporate design, working with businesses to help design their office spaces.

Initially, my design work was just about providing a solution to a client's request. However, I wanted to shape their workspaces so that, when employees showed up, they could be their best, do their best work, and easily accomplish their goals.

Leaders would share their company's goals and biggest obstacles with me—things like high sick leave, high turnover, missed deadlines, and large training expenses. I would then do a workplace analysis to identify where improvements were needed for efficiency within teams and across the organization. I interviewed team members and various employees to find out firsthand what was preventing them from doing their jobs well and loving it, what systems were missing for them, and what workflow processes could be added.

I'd combine the information from my analysis to create a design concept and then design the spaces—the offices, conference rooms, break rooms, entrances—in a way conducive to great overall workflow. As a result, projects were more successful. Individuals loved their jobs, loved coming to work, and got promotions. Teams hit deadlines and were able to take on new projects. Bottom lines were boosted, and everyone was happy.

It was all rooted in knowing how people needed to be set up behind the scenes to work well and be efficient. That's when I fell in love with systems and processes.

With my love of systems and processes, I could easily understand the business side of things when I started my coaching business, just as much as I could understand the coaching skills. I dove deep into understanding systems and processes at granular levels. I knew they were a big key to everything in a business working smoother and a big contributor for desired outcomes to happen naturally. The better the system, the quicker the results.

It was my love of systems and my mission for helping coaches remove the burdens and distractions behind the scenes in their businesses that sparked the creation of The Coaches Console System. I knew coaches loved coaching. I also knew coaches were not as well versed in business. Creating a software platform that included all the systems a coaching practice needed in one place removed the overwhelm from business, making it doable and even fun.

PILLAR 8: IMPLEMENTING BUSINESS OPERATIONS

Why are systems important? Stick with me. I can see your eyes starting to glaze over. My team laughs at me when I say, "Systems are sexy." But it's true, they are. By leveraging systems and processes, you're taking something seemingly complex and making it simple and doable. When you can bring organization and efficiency to the complex, you create freedom and flow—heck yeah, that's sexy!

How you implement the back end of your business during the amateur phase will make all the difference. You can either set yourself up to be reactive and struggle, or be proactive, freeing up your time and energy and increasing your confidence. The choice is yours. How you implement the back end of your business will either fuel overwhelm or create flow in your business.

Key Components for Implementing Professional Business Operations

Let's explore important differences in how amateurs and professionals approach this pillar. Understanding these distinctions can significantly inform your growth in this area.

1. Approach
    - *Amateurs* are often reactionary, addressing issues as they arise. This results in their back-end operations being patched or cobbled together.
    - *Professionals* take a proactive approach. They set up systems and processes in advance to ensure efficiency and a seamless client experience.

2. Systems and Scalability
   - *Amateurs* may not have established comprehensive systems for their back-end operations. They might rely on manual, time-consuming processes for tasks like client management, scheduling, and payment processing. Their manual approach prohibits them from working with a larger number of clients, capping their revenue potential.
   - *Professionals* typically have well-established systems for various aspects of their business that are both effective in the early stages of their business and easy to scale, allowing them to accommodate a larger client base while often working fewer hours.
3. Automation
   - *Amateurs* may not leverage software and tools to streamline tasks or enhance the client experience. Automation is usually minimal or nonexistent.
   - *Professionals* know that automation is a key component to their back-end operations. They use software and tools to automate redundant tasks like client onboarding, appointment scheduling, and payment processing. In bringing automation to their back end, they free up their time to focus on doing more revenue-generating activities and more of what they love.

PILLAR 8: IMPLEMENTING BUSINESS OPERATIONS

4. Technology Integration
   - *Amateurs* have little to no technology integration, as their focus is on manual processes.
   - *Professionals* recognize the efficiency of implementing a unified technology solution that seamlessly handles all aspects of their business back end, so they're not wasting time, energy, or resources on platforms that lack effective integration.

The Critical Point

Often, the first questions and concerns I hear from newer coaches are "Where do I start?" and "What should I do first, and then next?" and "Melinda, I feel like I'm scattered all over the place. I don't know what to do. I'm so overwhelmed."

It's understandable. Your enthusiasm for coaching and passion for serving others, combined with your excitement for doing this thing you love, catapulted you straight into asking, "Where can I find people to coach?! How can I get clients to coach?"

That's the wrong question to ask. Well, actually, it's not the wrong question. You're just asking it too early.

It's not your fault, especially if you've never had your own business before. Most coaches come from the employee mindset where you're great at a thing, you do that thing, and you get paid for that thing. As an employee, you only have to think about that one thing in order to do a good job. However, having your own business takes more than an employee mindset.

When you dive straight into asking, "How do I get clients?" you miss a critical point in your business and catapult yourself into "Oh crap, now what?" syndrome. Let's say that you learn from a mentor that you need online scheduling to make it easy for prospects to book a call with you. So you scramble and get a scheduling app in place. Then, early on, you talk with a potential client, and they actually say *yes* to hiring you. You call your coach and say, "Oh crap, they said yes, now what?!" and you scramble to get things in place so they can complete some basic forms and get started with you. Maybe you set up a contact resource management software to organize your contacts and their information.

Then as you keep going, you learn from someone else that you need an easy way for clients to pay you. So you scramble again and get an online shopping cart in place to sell your packages online. You keep throwing yourself down the reactive path, piecemealing the back end of your business together. Hello, overwhelm!

You're barely getting started and you've already had to patch three different technologies together just to accomplish the basic business tasks. And you're not alone. One of our students described her business as being "held together by spit balls and duct tape," while another student called her business "a giant pile of spaghetti."

If a coach continues on this path, they could easily end up with about seven to nine different technologies they have to use just to find clients, convert them, coach them, and get paid by them. Having to manage that many technologies can be daunting, and certainly fuels overwhelm. (The Coaches

PILLAR 8: IMPLEMENTING BUSINESS OPERATIONS

Console System combines all of these functionalities into one seamless platform.)

That reactive approach is the root cause of overwhelm. It's why so many coaches don't like the idea of leveraging technology to streamline their business; the tech stack that's been patched together feels more complex than just doing all the business tasks manually. All because you whizzed right past that critical point that I call the Foundation Phase.

At that moment when a coach first makes a commitment to starting a business doing what they love while making good money (and they know they want to be more than a hobbyist or an amateur), ideally, they take a moment to ask a different kind of question, one a business owner asks: What needs to be set up behind the scenes so I can:

1. grow my audience and contact list consistently,
2. convert prospects into paying clients consistently,
3. easily onboard new clients and feel confident I can deliver what I promised,
4. automate the referral process so it's easier to get more clients?

The answers to these questions ensure you're taking a *proactive*, professional approach to setting up your business. Now you can be intentional about learning what you need behind the scenes so you can streamline and simplify your business and prepare it for growth right out of the gate.

The Coaching Business Roadmap to Success

To help coaches easily take the proactive professional approach, I created The Coaching Business Roadmap to Success: a one-page infographic that outlines the path every professional business must follow, no matter what size you want your business to be. The Roadmap is organized into five phases:

Phase 0: Foundation Phase
Phase I: Coaching Client Quick-Start
Phase II: Optimizing Conversions and Mastering Enrollment
Phase III: Leveraging
Phase IV: Scaling

Within each phase, there are action items, which are organized into success systems, to implement behind the scenes. In the early phases, as you're an amateur, you start simple and do the best you can, with what you have, from where you are. As you evolve through the phases, you optimize for better results. If you want to work with only a handful of clients and earn a modest income, then you must still do these things to thrive; you'll just do them on a smaller scale.

As an analogy, think about putting together a jigsaw puzzle; you always look first at the box cover photo to first know what you're creating. Then as you pick up each piece, you can refer to the box photo for guidance as to where that

PILLAR 8: IMPLEMENTING BUSINESS OPERATIONS

piece will fit. Having the photo makes it easier (and more fun) to put the pieces together. This Roadmap serves as the box photo for your business.

The Coaching Business Roadmap to Success

Visit the Additional Resources section in the back of this book to download the Professional Coaching Business Tool Kit and a detailed copy of this Roadmap.

When you learn what is needed behind the scenes, you can put your attention on the right actions at the right times to get quick results. You can create systems and processes that help you feel confident delivering what you promise while working smarter, not harder. And you can find one comprehensive technology (like The Coaches Console) right from the beginning that handles everything without having to build a complex tech stack.

Once your business back end is built out (even in a simple fashion), then you can go back and ask the question, "How do I get clients?" At that point, everything is ready when prospects and clients start coming in!

It reminds me of a paraphrase of the quote in the movie, *Field of Dreams*—Build it and they will come. Many amateurs mistakenly think, *If I just build my business and put up an "open for business" sign, clients will magically appear.* In business, it's not "build it and they will come." It's "build it, then you'll feel more confident to put yourself out there and connect with potential clients in a professional way." *Then* they'll come.

The Magic of Systems and Processes

First of all, let's actually define what a "system" is. A system is an organized group of elements that outlines how you do something in your business to achieve your overall goals. It's something that helps your business run.

The processes are all the steps you carry out in order to make any given system work most efficiently.

The technology is the tool that can simplify, streamline, or automate the processes that make up the system.

Systems help you streamline and automate the redundant tasks behind the scenes, freeing up your time and energy and creating a consistent experience for your prospects and clients. As a result, you dial up your confidence and quiet your fears and doubts. At the same time, you increase your clients' confidence as well.

PILLAR 8: IMPLEMENTING BUSINESS OPERATIONS

The Seven Success Systems Every Professional Coaching Business Needs

As complex as your coaching business may feel at times, there are really only seven success systems you need to pay attention to:

Branding – Using messaging and images that generate awareness with your ideal audience.

List Building – Capturing leads who are interested in the transformation your services provide.

Converting – Guiding those interested in making a purchasing decision.

Enrolling – Inviting them to make a buying decision and signing up paying clients.

Supporting – Delivering what was promised so clients achieve desired outcomes.

Referring – Engaging strategic partners who can introduce you to new clients.

Leveraging – Working with more people in less time through group programs, courses, memberships, and other models.

You'll find each of these success systems in the different phases of your business evolution—they just exist to different degrees. And the way in which you maneuver through implementing the Roadmap will make *all* the difference between feeling burdened versus liberated by your business.

The Real Reason I See Coaches Struggle in Their Business

When I see coaches struggling in their businesses, it's often not because of their coaching skills. It's not even because they're bad at marketing or sales.

The reason most coaches struggle is because their businesses (the back-end infrastructures) have become so complex that they can't work with any sort of consistency. If they can't find a way to streamline this complexity, they typically end up reinventing the wheel for every client and working way harder than necessary, limiting the number of clients they're able to take, or giving up.

When I see a coach struggling with not being able to grow their list, or they tell me they hate selling, or they can't figure out how to make it all work—those are *symptoms* of complexity.

You don't have a coaching skills problem, or even a marketing or sales problem. You have an implementation problem. The seven success systems exist to make implementation easy. Otherwise, you're left with a sporadic, reactive, make-shit-up-as-you-go approach. Your business will be left with holes and gaps and missing elements. Like a bucket of water with holes in it, your business will be leaking leads, leaking clients, leaking revenue, and you'll suffer from lost opportunities.

The more of these systems you have in place, the more confident and professional you'll feel. The more confident you feel behind the scenes in your business, the more confident you'll feel as a coach. You can then stop doubting your

PILLAR 8: IMPLEMENTING BUSINESS OPERATIONS

skills, services, and calling. The imposter syndrome will melt away and you can let your light shine. Then you'll be more confident to put yourself out there.

The key is to know the details of what strategies, steps, and materials you need to have in place for each of the seven success systems within each business phase. Know how the processes and systems interconnect. And then start doing each thing at the right moment, in the right sequence. Adjust and optimize each system as your coaching business grows (to whatever degree you want it to grow), so that your business, marketing, and sales strategies are always in line with the phase of business you're in. Use the Roadmap as your guide through each phase.

Going Pro Tip

Implementing the seven success structures will go a long way to making your business professional while reducing your overwhelm. But implementing each one is not all there is to it! It's how these individual systems and technology platforms are connected and integrated, working together, that simplifies your coaching business and makes it easier and quicker to get sustainable, scalable results. Without integration, the technologies you use behind the scenes can get so complex that overwhelm creeps back in.

After spending months on website creation, Rita faced unexpected hurdles just before her planned launch. Wanting to add a simple opt-in form led to a shocking discovery—her website platform didn't handle follow-up emails. Annoyed, she purchased a recommended platform and navigated its learning curve. Needing an online calendar link in follow-up messages, she encountered another roadblock after the support person told her that feature wasn't included in their platform, requiring a third software purchase.

After additional testing, she discovered issues between the website and email apps. Frustrated, Rita eventually hired help, resulting in longer delays and more expenses. Despite her initial excitement, Rita's enthusiasm for her launch dwindled due to the tech struggles and hassles dealing with multiple platforms.

Integration means all the technology is talking to each other and working together without you having to manage it all, just like a series of gears interlocks with each one moving the next. But integration doesn't happen by magic. *What* you integrate matters just as much as *how* you integrate it. You need your back-office infrastructure to integrate all the best practices of a thriving, professional business so it becomes a well-oiled machine.

When you're aware of the Roadmap to Success up front, you know *what* to create. Then you can get one technology to easily integrate everything you need in your business. That's why I created The Coaches Console back in 2004, to be the most full-featured, fully integrated platform designed specifically for coaching businesses!

Going Pro Checklist

- Review the Coaching Business Roadmap to Success and determine which business phase you're currently in. (Hint: if anything is missing from one of the phases, you don't get to skip ahead to the next phase yet.)

- Review the seven success systems and determine which ones are missing or incomplete in your business.
- Make a list of the redundant tasks that can be automated in your business.
- Implement one integrated technology platform to streamline your business.

Oracle Card Exercise
#45 The Seer

The Seer represents the capacity to reach beyond the obvious details of life, into the Hidden Realms where information is available to those with the discernment to perceive it. . . . The Seer knows truth, always seeks truth beyond all else, and sees reality as it truly is without judgment.

The Seer has arrived now to challenge you to get out of denial and begin telling yourself the truth about your situation. Wishful thinking will not make what you desire happen when you're refusing to see things as they are. The truth may hurt, but it will set you free to claim the bounty that is waiting for you to notice it. . . .

Why is this the perfect message for you, right now, as it relates to this chapter?

Take a few moments of quiet reflection time to journal what the message means to you:

_____

_____

_____

_____

Favorite Frames

Take a moment to write down your top takeaways, key learnings, aha moments, and insights that stood out the most. By identifying these, you deepen your commitment to becoming a professional.

Here are some of my favorite frames to recap some of the key points in this chapter:

- Having your own business takes more than an employee mindset.
- You don't have a coaching skills problem, or even a marketing or sales problem. You have an implementation problem.
- Systems are sexy—they take the complexity in business and make it simple and doable.

PILLAR 8: IMPLEMENTING BUSINESS OPERATIONS

Feel free to add your own favorite frames in the following space!

Sustainability in Business:
PERFORMING AT HIGH LEVELS WITHOUT BURNING OUT

> Give up the delusion that burnout is the inevitable cost of success.
> —Arianna Huffington

> Dear Stress, I would like a divorce. Please understand it is not you, it is me.
> —Thomas E. Rojo

In the year leading up to the first launch of my signature program, I kept a diligent eye on others in the industry, watching their launches closely from behind the scenes and learning everything I could about how to organize and manage all the moving parts and pieces of the promotion.

Sometimes I would hear a colleague say, "I've been up for forty-eight hours straight trying to get this copy written in time." Then they'd complete it minutes before it was supposed to be emailed or added to a sales page. Or I'd hear things like, "I haven't gotten out of my pajamas and haven't eaten in days; this launch has consumed me." Crunch culture abounded. And while these tactics usually resulted in successful launches (multiple six figures), I'd then watch those overworked leaders plummet—one got so sick that he was out for a week and missed the start of program fulfillment. In another case, I watched two stressed-out business partners completely attack each other in horrible ways.

Over and over again I watched as folks would "love" the drama of their situation; they would take pride in their suffering in the name of having a great launch, reaching the point of depletion in the name of success.

Concurrently, I was studying about embracing the feminine—new ways of expressing myself and new approaches to pursuing pleasure, bearing in mind that self-care was the greatest act of self-love. I didn't want to blindly follow the patriarchal path to success at any cost. I wanted success, *and* I wanted to experience it in a way that lit me up and left me overflowing rather than depleted.

Those two things—hearing how my colleagues were taking pride in their depletion, combined with my immense desire to pursue a different path—led me to decide then and there that, if we were going to do a launch, it was *never* going to be like what all the other guys were doing. I wanted us to be able to create success while taking care of ourselves. I wanted to incorporate fun and joy through the whole experience. That was the origin of a nickname that's stuck with me through much of my career—the Queen of Self-Care.

In the journey of entrepreneurship, the desire and drive for success often comes with the risk of burnout if you're not careful. The work you're doing is a calling; you love doing it and want to do it more than anything. But the journey to being a professional coach with a thriving business isn't worth it if you end up resenting your calling or sacrificing your physical or mental health, or other important parts of your life.

I'm dedicating an entire chapter to this topic, because in my twenty years of coaching coaches and building a multimillion-dollar coaching business, what I've included in this chapter is my hidden advantage.

You have read about the eight pillars of professionalism. To nurture your success, you have to be intentional about *how* you navigate those pillars and how you take care of yourself along the way. What follows is meant to be integrated throughout your entire journey.

Key Components for Cultivating Sustainability

Let's explore important differences in how amateurs and professionals approach this pillar. Understanding these distinctions can significantly inform your growth in this area.

1. Approach
   - *Amateurs* may view self-care as an afterthought or something to consider only when they're overwhelmed, stressed, or sick. It's a reactionary response.
   - *Professionals* view self-care as a strategic component of their overall success. It's an integrated and intentional part of their routine, recognized as essential for sustained high performance. For them, it's a proactive strategy to avoid burnout.

2. Understanding
   - *Amateurs* will have a limited understanding of self-care, focusing primarily on physical well-being.
   - *Professionals* grasp the holistic nature of self-care, encompassing the six different types of self-care.
3. Time
   - *Amateurs* might perceive self-care as a time-consuming task on their to-do list or a luxury they can't afford due to the demands of starting a business.
   - *Professionals* understand the value of self-care and prioritize it within their schedule. They recognize how it enhances their ability to perform at their best.

The Path Less Traveled

There's a cliché that says it's not about the destination, it's about the journey. I believe both destination and journey are equally important. It's about the destination because, when that destiny is reached, new opportunities become available to you that didn't exist before. It's also about who you become on the way to that destination. Self-care is *how* you'll actually traverse the journey and make it to the destination in a way that honors all parts of you. (And by the way, I'm not just talking about meditation, massages, and manicures.)

SUSTAINABILITY IN BUSINESS

It is possible to create a business beyond your wildest dreams while also creating a lifestyle beyond your wildest dreams, without burning out or sacrificing parts of yourself in the name of your calling—this chapter unlocks that secret.

The Road to Burnout

Formally, the World Health Organization classifies burnout as an occupational phenomenon, not a medical condition. It's defined as "a syndrome conceptualized as resulting from chronic workplace stress that has not been successfully managed."

I really resonated with the less formal definition given during episode #41 of my *Just Between Coaches* podcast, when Michelle Falzon described it this way: "Burnout is losing the ability to do the thing you're meant to do with joy."

In that episode, Michelle painted a clear picture as to why burnout can happen so quickly. The typical approach to creating (whether you're building your business, writing a book, or embarking on any project), is to first learn, research, gather, and collect whatever information is necessary for that project. From there, most folks immediately dive straight into creating, focusing on the output and implementation—the doing, the tasks, actions, and activities to bring that project to reality. Learn—Do. Learn—Do. Learn—Do . . . It's a short path, but it is dangerously addictive and potentially exhausting. It's the fast path to burnout.

Early on, this constant learn-do path feels productive and good because you're getting a lot of stuff done. But it's not sustainable. By the time you realize that, though, you've created a deeply defined rut of learn-do and it's hard to propel yourself out.

A More Sustainable Model

I want to briefly bring back the Create Without Burnout model I shared in the "How to Navigate This Book" chapter at the beginning of this book. Michelle's model not only enhances sustainability, but also taps into your creativity on a deeper level, creating a sense of effortless flow.

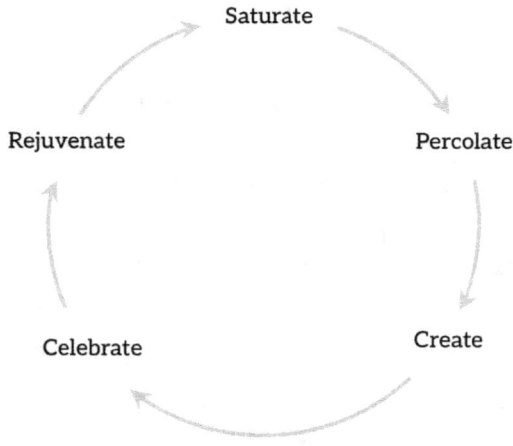

The Five Stages of the Create Without Burnout Cycle

The learn-do path is like only focusing on the Saturate and Create parts of Michelle's model. But there's more to this picture. Making sure to incorporate the often-overlooked

SUSTAINABILITY IN BUSINESS

Percolate, Celebrate, and Rejuvenate phases is what helps to create a sustainable business and a sustainable you. Following this cycle allows you to be a high achiever and top performer with high expectations, without overworking or reaching exhaustion.

When I began sharing this concept of integrating self-care into business with the Director of Operations of a multimillion-dollar company, she was very resistant at first. In her determined efforts to launch massive promotions, meet high demands, and hit big goals, she couldn't see how taking time away from her already busy schedule could in any way help her avoid burning out. She was stuck on a fast-driving cycle of production, trying to hold it all up so that it (or she) didn't come crashing down.

What she learned over time was that self-care was actually performance coaching. She said, "Ultimately, for me, the key learning was that self-care was actually a tool to help me level up my performance; it wasn't about creating 'me time.' That's what really motivated me to implement."

She began to see how by integrating different types of self-care into her daily activities, she gave herself fuel to achieve her high goals while still having high expectations. In this way, everything she did became easier and more fun.

So often when I use the phrase "self-care," people start thinking about massages or meditation. And while there's nothing wrong with either massages or meditation, self-care goes further than that. The Create Without Burnout Cycle builds in self-care throughout your entire routine.

Self-Care Myths and Misconceptions

Before we get too far into exploring this secret advantage, we need to first debunk the misunderstandings. Some of the common *myths* say that self-care is:

1. **A reward.** Many view self-care as an after-the-fact treat—a reward for working hard.

2. **A luxury.** Self-care is often viewed as a nice way to treat oneself to something special; a selfish indulgence, reserved for special occasions (like a trip to the spa on vacation).

3. **Impossible to schedule.** Entrepreneurs are often so busy that they can't even see when to add self-care tasks to their to-do list.

4. **No part of business.** Taking care of yourself is for your personal time—if you have any to spare.

5. **A last resort.** Self-care often only becomes a priority when it's forced upon you by chronic stress or illness—the flu sets in and you're forced to rest, a migraine kicks in and you're forced to curl up in a dark room, an injury occurs and you're forced to stay off your feet for a week.

By letting go of these misconceptions, you can appreciate self-care for what it really is: the intentional practice of taking an active role in protecting your own well-being and happiness. Embracing this perspective allows you to leverage self-care as a strategic tool to pursue your calling and business while maintaining high expectations, all while infusing your journey with joy.

Give from the Overflow

Imagine your energy, attention, and creativity as a pitcher of water, with each project or responsibility represented by a cup beneath it. The goal is to continually fill up your pitcher to tackle these tasks effectively: "I've filled up my energy, and now I'm ready to dive into my projects."

As you engage in various projects or assist others, visualize the water pouring from your full pitcher into the corresponding cups below. You create an email campaign—water is poured into one of the cups. A team member needs your assistance—more water is poured into another cup. You're in the middle of a launch with a lot of moving parts and pieces you need to oversee—more water is poured out.

Each endeavor draws from your energy reserve until your pitcher is empty. To keep going, you need to stop and refill your pitcher. It's akin to taking a break or going on vacation to rejuvenate and replenish your energy—which most busy entrepreneurs don't do (see preceding Self-Care Myths and Misconceptions section), so they keep giving from the place of depletion. Would you get on an airplane to fly across the country when the fuel tank is empty? No, me neither.

People who don't want to continuously sputter on fumes generally feel like they have to go through a stop-and-go cycle of expending and refilling—working to exhaustion and then taking a long break. But the constant stop and go can be draining.

Now, envision an alternative scenario where your pitcher is connected to an endless water source. The pitcher remains consistently full, allowing the water to overflow into the cups below without interruption into your various responsibilities—be it projects, family, or personal pursuits. The water continuously flows out, while simultaneously replenishing itself.

In this scenario, the cups representing your commitments are always being filled. The idea is to give from the overflow, ensuring that you never have to stop to recharge. Instead of sporadically refueling, you're consistently fueling yourself as you go. This approach enables you to give more to your endeavors, be it coaching clients, managing campaigns, or engaging with audiences, without risking depletion.

Bear in mind: the degree to which your actions and activity increase, is the degree to which your self-care must also increase.

Rhythmic Renewal

Suneel Gupta, author of *Everyday Dharma: 8 Essential Practices for Finding Success and Joy in Everything You Do*, suggests practicing rhythmic renewal. "Instead of waiting for vacations or long weekends to get periods of rest, high performers take frequent focused breaks every single day," he says. "The average high performer takes around eight breaks every single day."

Gupta recommends the "55:5 model," which is working for 55 minutes and then taking five minutes of rest. "The break can be anything from sipping a cup of coffee to listening to music or meditating," he says. "Anything deliberately non-productive. Each of those five minutes will make the other 55 minutes more productive, creative and reflective. You'll have more energy for yourself and the people around you."

In an interview with Katie Couric about his book, Gupta shared this about his 55:5 model:

> You want to take in pure rest, and this is hard for people because our instinct is that when we're overwhelmed, we try to squeeze as much juice out of every minute of every day. And so the idea of shrinking your hour by five minutes doesn't feel immediately palatable to people. But what the science tells us is that each of those five minutes is going to make the other 55 minutes far more effective, far more productive, far more creative, far more collaborative.
>
> It's easy to think that the people who do the most are the ones sitting at their desks the longest, but I don't think that's true. I think they're the people who were able to maintain their energy over time, the ones with good work and rest ethics.

One thing I know to be true—what you schedule in your calendar tells me what your priorities are. So make sure you're scheduling in both work activities (meetings, project work, etc.) and rest and renewal activities. Block self-care off on your calendar so you can honor your commitment to be your best so you can do your best.

Reframing Self-Care

Self-care simply refers to activities that bring you joy, pleasure, and happiness. It will be unique to each person. Your actions of self-care protect your joy! To further clarify what self-care is, let's look at what it's not. Whatever actions or activities you engage in, they should not cause harm or stress tomorrow. Self-care is not unmindful indulgence.

Let's say you're going for a fun night out. Everything starts off great—you're having drinks, enjoying the night, and dancing away. You're having such a blast that you keep ordering more drinks—a second, third, and even a fourth.

Guess what happens the next morning? You have to cancel your appointments and deal with a brutal hangover. When you say yes to pleasure today, it shouldn't cause harm to tomorrow. You can stop after a drink or two so you can start the next day well-rested and full of stories from a fun time with friends.

The Neuroscience of Self-Care

Now that you have a clearer understanding of the *what* and *why* behind self-care, let's dig deeper into the science.

When stress levels are high, the stress hormones, such as adrenaline or cortisol, that are released into your bloodstream may alter your brain's ability to process information.

You may know this as brain fog, or difficulty focusing and concentrating.

When you are intentional about engaging in self-care practices, you can reduce stress hormone levels and increase the happy hormones—endorphins, serotonin, oxytocin, and dopamine.

Endorphins are responsible for that "runner's high," and the benefits can last for six to eight hours. Serotonin governs whether you're operating from a sense of calm and focus or from anxiety and fear. Oxytocin lowers anxiety. Dopamine gives you feelings of pleasure, satisfaction, and motivation. Taking care of yourself triggers these happy hormones in ways that build you up instead of breaking you down. They keep you going when things feel difficult; they help reduce the overwhelm.

Practicing self-care can increase productivity. And as you reset your nervous system and bring equilibrium to your hormone levels, you start to see brain fog clear, experience an ability to refocus, and have renewed energy levels. When you are more focused and energized, you are better equipped to serve your clients, manage projects, and still have time for the things you love outside of work.

Neuroscientists have ways of scanning your system and brain for signatures of pessimism or optimism. After just fifteen minutes of self-care activities, these signatures change. You may already understand all this. You may be nodding your head up and down saying, "I totally get it, Melinda." But beware, because our actions don't often align with our brains.

Making Choices to Support Desired Outcomes

Often the reason folks don't do what they know to be helpful has to do with priorities, boundaries, and choices.

By nature, coaches are all about serving and helping others. That puts the emphasis on others, with yourself taking a back seat (even more true for women). But when you can prioritize yourself, that generally allows you to be of greater service to others. When you remind yourself regularly of *why* you're practicing self-care, it becomes easier to practice healthy habits.

Taking care of yourself can also be challenging if boundaries are blurry. Boundaries allow you to communicate your needs and expectations to your friends, family, colleagues, or clients. Setting a boundary that allows you to conserve your energy and protect your physical and mental health is vital to helping you be the best business owner and coach you can be.

The act of simply saying no is powerful. What do you need to say no to so you can say yes to opportunities or experiences that are more aligned with your goals and bigger visions?

Operating in a depleted, reactive mode facilitates short-term, immediate choices and short-term, sporadic results. In order to make good choices, it's important to ask: Who is being affected if I make this choice? What is the positive and negative ripple effect of this choice? How will this choice make my business easier or harder in the future?

Clarifying your priorities, establishing aligned boundaries, and consistently making choices that support your desired outcomes create a smoother journey that's a lot more fun.

The Self-Care Flywheel

Six Types of Self-Care

To aid you in fueling all parts of yourself for your grand business adventure, taking care of yourself goes beyond the physical (massages) and spiritual (meditation). There are six common categories of self-care. Each contribute to reducing feelings of anxiety, minimizing feelings of frustration, improving concentration and creativity, and boosting your happiness. They include:

1. **Emotional.** Activities that help you connect, process, and reflect on a full range of emotions.
2. **Practical.** Activities to help prevent further stress, such as creating a budget or organizing a room.

3. **Physical.** Activities to help your body keep up with your goal/vision/desire.
4. **Mental.** Activities to keep your intellect sharp and your creativity flowing.
5. **Social.** Activities to encourage compassion, empathy, and connectedness.
6. **Spiritual.** Activities to help keep perspective on that which is greater than you and to keep the magic alive.

Examples of Self-Care

- Walk in nature
- Massage
- Healthy diet
- Dance breaks
- Afternoon nap
- Morning ritual
- Meditation
- Manicure
- Oracle cards
- Acts of anonymous good
- Essential oils
- Gratitudes
- Ride a bike

- Lunch with a friend
- Time with animals
- Sharing celebrations/wins
- Breathwork
- Fresh flowers
- Martial arts
- Workout
- Organizing your desk
- Doing puzzles
- Savoring chocolate
- Creating a budget
- Sound healing

- Laughing
- Reading a book
- Painting
- Going to music gigs
- Hiking
- Playing with your dog or cat
- Earthing (grounding)
- Playing a musical instrument
- Hydrating
- Fishing
- Fixing something
- Journaling

_____   _____   _____

_____   _____   _____

I could keep going on and on with additional examples, but I think you get the idea. I've even left space in the table for you to add your own. Whatever actions, activities, or experiences you add, just remember that just because a behavior is good for you or fun doesn't automatically make it self-care.

What self-care is for one person, may not be for another. Really listen to your body; take a moment to check in, intentionally paying attention to what brings you relief, rejuvenation, and renewal. Those are the items and activities to integrate into your daily routines.

Identifying Your Baseline Self-Care Plan

Now that you've scanned through the self-care examples, go back through your last two to three days. What self-care activities are you already doing? List them out.

Many don't even realize just how much self-care is already baked into their schedule. Because they don't have the framing of self-care, they only see these different actions as more tasks on their to-do list and see them as time-sucks. But when you shift your perspective and see these same actions and activities in a different light … don't look now, but you're already integrating self-care.

Bringing intention to what you're already doing is a first step in creating your baseline self-care plan. What self-care tasks do you need to put on your calendar in the course of a normal workday?

For me, it means sitting down at my altar each morning with my singing bowls and oracle deck. It also means reading my TUT.com "Notes from the Universe" daily email. Each of those activities helps to get my mind and spirit aligned before I begin my workday. It also means I'm having a green smoothie each morning to fuel my body. There are frequent dance breaks with the team, and time spent walking or training/playing with my dog. This is just in the course of a normal day. This is part of my baseline plan.

What is your "normal"?

Creating Your Project Self-Care Plan

Next, you can begin to create an enhanced self-care plan for when projects come up that demand increased output. Remember to factor in both the tasks you *want* to do related to that project and the tasks that *have* to be done.

One of my single girlfriends loathed cleaning her house. Hiring a housekeeper wasn't an option. She prioritized her pleasure and happiness, so she decided she'd vacuum the house while wearing her sexy lingerie and her spiked heels. She didn't mind doing it so much after that.

For the tasks you have to do (but may not be that excited about doing), ask yourself:

- How can I do this in a way that brings me pleasure?

- What else do I need to make this more enjoyable?
- Who can help me make this more fun?

When you add intention and pleasure, you transform the tedious into a treasure.

Not only can you create a plan for the way in which you complete the tasks in your business (or life), you can also create specific self-care plans for projects, launches, client-fulfillment retreats, or other significant aspects of your business.

Remember earlier in the chapter, when I said that as your activities ramp up, your self-care must also ramp up at the same level?

Twice a year The Coaches Console team does a big launch promotion in which we open enrollments to our signature online training and coaching program. It's an intense three weeks in which we facilitate several live webinars plus a three-day virtual live event. It takes months of planning, with each team member handling an increased workload.

We've been doing launches since 2014, and every year, just as the planning is about to begin, the team and I create our launch self-care plans. We each identify how we'll ramp up our self-care activities to protect our energy as schedules get busier and tasks grow exponentially. We incorporate as many of the different self-care categories as we can to protect our fun, joy, and creativity throughout the process. It allows us to create complex campaigns without burning out, and have fun along the way.

For one team member, that meant more time with her horses. For others it meant body work (massages, chiropractor, acupuncture), and for others it meant more walks outside or a favorite brand of chocolate within reach. It didn't matter what we did, just so long as it protected our joy and kept our energy up as we were engaged in a lot of output in a concentrated amount of time.

What Is your Project Self-Care Plan?

To create your own project self-care plan, answer the following questions:

- What will you do the week prior to your project starting?
- Which self-care categories will support you to build up your energy reserves?
- What will you do as the project kicks off?
- Which self-care activities will help you navigate the actual project creation time (when you're creating, building, or implementing the project)?
- What types of self-care will aid you as you come to the end of your project?
- What will you do once the project has concluded?

When you bring sustainability practices to all aspects of your business and life, you adopt a professional approach to setting up and running your business. You can be of greater service to your clients, and you set yourself up to scale to whatever degree you want your business and impact to be.

Going Pro Tip

During our Coaches Console launches, one thing that helped me give fully and completely to our audience was to bookend our launch with two critical acts of self-care. My massage therapist is a miracle worker. She integrates massage, cupping, magnets, and crystals to really work the muscles. When I knew a launch was coming up, I scheduled two massages, one just before the launch was scheduled to start, and another at the very end.

Knowing I had bookended this high-intensity period with great self-care helped me not be concerned about giving to the point of depletion throughout the launch. I knew I could give everything I had because I had rejuvenation already built into my plan. I never feared giving too much, never got exhausted, never hit the proverbial wall. I flowed through it all, maintaining good, healthy energy. I could better serve my team and my clients.

Going Pro Checklist

- Identify self-care practices you're already doing and create your baseline plan.
- Circle the different self-care examples you most resonate with (making sure there's at least one for each of the six categories).

- Create your project self-care plan and share it with your coach, team, or colleagues.
- Integrate Gupta's 55:5 model and prioritize by scheduling it in your calendar.

Oracle Card Exercise
#28 Jaguar

The Jaguar is the protector of all life. . . . In times of fear she brings courage and certainty. . . . She moves gracefully through the jungle, relishing the abundance of the rainforest, fearless and at ease. . . .

Jaguar calls you to explore beyond the walls that confine you, to go outside your normal routine, to push your limits and boundaries. She is delivering an invitation from your own future to investigate the unknown, to venture into the mystery and the dark places you have been reluctant to explore. Toss all caution to the wind! Know that your Jaguar instinct will serve you well.

Why is this the perfect message for you, right now, as it relates to this chapter?

Take a few moments of quiet reflection time to journal what the message means to you:

_____

_____

_____

_____

Favorite Frames

Take a moment to write down your top takeaways, key learnings, aha moments, and insights that stood out the most. By identifying these, you deepen your commitment to becoming a professional.

Here are some of my favorite frames to recap some of the key points in this chapter:

- Nurture success and be intentional about *how* you navigate the pillars. Take care of yourself along the way so you don't burnout.
- The definition of burnout: "losing the ability to do the thing you're meant to do with joy."
- Create a project self-care plan. When you add intention and pleasure, you transform the tedious into a treasure.

SUSTAINABILITY IN BUSINESS

Feel free to add your own favorite frames in the following space!

Conclusion
PRACTICE MAKES PROGRESS

> What lies behind us and what lies before us
> are tiny matters compared to what lies within us.
> —Henry Stanley Haskins

It's the last day of our live event. I'm standing on stage teaching my Coaching Business Roadmap to Success. When we get to the Q&A portion, some of the questions share a similar theme. Despite aspiring to professionalism, a lot of my students struggle with negative self-talk, making it very difficult to implement the new systems, processes, and strategies we teach.

Then Lori, our coach team leader, stands up and shares a way to combat negative self-talk. "You need to practice saying a new, positive message out loud until it becomes as easy as saying 'pass the salt.' The more you say something out loud, the more normal it feels."

"Pass the salt" has become a signature phrase that I, my coach team, and our students use when trying to convey how simple something new can become, if we just let it. As I mentioned in an earlier chapter, just because something is awkward doesn't mean it's wrong. It's just different and it takes practice.

Coaches who have made the conscious choice to go beyond the level of a hobbyist and establish a business often see themselves as professionals, yet their behaviors may not yet align with this perception. They don't always think or act like true professionals. This lack of professionalism often keeps their business overly complicated, triggering all kinds of negative self-talk. The misalignment keeps them stuck, hiding behind their fears and doubts.

Swift progress toward professionalism, though, cultivates deep trust in those around you and attracts the right type of clients willing to invest in your services. This level of professionalism not only ensures a successful business doing what you love, but also unlocks your full potential while reaping financial rewards.

This book has navigated through the pillars necessary for coaches to confidently transition from amateur to professional, making the business-building journey as straightforward as saying "pass the salt."

We've accomplished a lot on our journey, and this book is just the starting point. While your business will be here for years, maybe decades to come, impacting countless lives, it is dynamic and ever-evolving. As your clients evolve, as your business model shifts, as your business goals change, revisit and refine the pillars outlined in this book. Use them to elevate your professionalism.

Remember, your business plan must include you too, and the sustainable practices and self-care tips provided should act as your fuel to serve others from a place of abundance. You can be of greater service to your clients when you're giving of the overflow and inviting Spirit into your work. In doing so, you set yourself up to scale to whatever degree you desire.

I'll leave you with a snippet from a favorite quote that was the inspiration for starting my coaching business:

> "... As we let our own light shine, we unconsciously give other people permission to do the same. As we're liberated from our own fear, our presence automatically liberates others."
> —Marianne Williamson

Operating in a professional manner as outlined in this book allows you to step into your confidence, boldly letting your light shine to pave the way for others to do the same.

Having your own business can be the most rewarding adventure of your life, one that not only creates an amazing life for you, but also helps those you serve create extraordinary lives as well. The ripple effect of your professionalism is exponential.

My husband always calls me the Pied Piper-ess for coaches. I love being the way-shower. I have loved being the messenger and way-shower for you on this adventure as you step into your full potential—both as a human in the playground of business and as a spiritual being in the playground of life. What an honor it's been.

To your prosperity beyond your wildest dreams,

XO Melinda

THE PROFESSIONAL COACH

Oracle Card Exercise
#52 Standstill

When Standstill appears, it is a symbol of pausing, the act of observation, and breathing space. It represents the benefits of temporary nonaction as well as what happens when one is stuck.

Time to get out of "analysis paralysis." Standstill invites you to turn within, breathe, and recognize this is the condition of the moment; it allows you the opportunity to bear witness to whatever is going on before movement resumes.

Why is this the perfect message for you, right now, as it relates to where you are on the path to becoming a professional?

_____

_____

_____

_____

THE COMPREHENSIVE GOING PRO CHECKLIST

Pillar 1: Expanding Commitment and Dedication

- ☐ Complete the Stair Step to Your *Why* statement.
- ☐ Write out what 100 percent commitment looks like to you.
- ☐ Share the "Always do your best" concept from don Miguel Ruiz's book *The Four Agreements* with at least three other people closest to you on this journey to deepen the promise to yourself to not confuse perfection with commitment.
- ☐ Identify your top three priorities.

Pillar 2: Defining Work Ethic

- ☐ Establish your work hours.
- ☐ Hang a "Please do not disturb. I'm on my way to my next $10K" sign on your office door or in your working area.
- ☐ Set up your dedicated workspace so it's clutter-free and inspiring.

- [ ] Complete the Clarity Quadrant for any business decision, big or small.

Pillar 3: Creating Your Unique Value Proposition

- [ ] Conduct market research interviews to gather the words and phrases your ideal client is using to describe their urgent needs and desired outcomes.
- [ ] Collect existing client feedback to better understand what clients most appreciate about working with you specifically.
- [ ] Create your Unique Value Proposition.
- [ ] Create your Five-Part Conversation.

Pillar 4: Establishing Accountability for Outcomes

- [ ] Define the space and tools a client needs in order for success to be inevitable.
- [ ] Prioritize a client-focused approach.
- [ ] Map out your Client Success Path.
- [ ] Establish your formal coaching agreement or terms of service that includes specific goal-setting frameworks and other key performance indicators.
- [ ] Provide an organized, secure, private client portal.

THE COMPREHENSIVE GOING PRO CHECKLIST

Pillar 5: Designing Delivery of Client Support

- ☐ Create your onboarding messages.
- ☐ Establish exquisite client support in your practice.
- ☐ Organize your clients in a private client portal.
- ☐ Leverage a software platform to track, manage, and interact with your clients.

Pillar 6: Setting Professional Pricing

- ☐ Rewire outdated money beliefs.
- ☐ Complete the Money Matrix exercise.
- ☐ Prioritize your financial well-being while ensuring that your clients receive substantial value in return.
- ☐ Establish result-based pricing for two packages.

Pillar 7: Managing Business Finances

- ☐ Increase your financial literacy by getting familiar and comfortable with the terms and concepts in business. Whether it's reading a book, playing the Cashflow board game, or talking with a colleague

about this topic, do something every week that expands your knowledge.
- ☐ Open a business bank account.
- ☐ Pay yourself.
- ☐ Create a simple budget.
- ☐ Create your cash flow report.
- ☐ Schedule a weekly meeting to review the numbers in your business.
- ☐ Identify a cause you would love to support when your profitability reaches a certain point.

Pillar 8: Implementing Business Operations

- ☐ Review the Coaching Business Roadmap to Success and determine which business phase you're currently in. (Hint: if anything is missing from one of the phases, you don't get to skip ahead to the next phase yet.)
- ☐ Review the seven success systems and determine which ones are missing or incomplete in your business.
- ☐ Make a list of the redundant tasks that can be automated in your business.
- ☐ Implement one integrated technology platform to streamline your business.

THE COMPREHENSIVE GOING PRO CHECKLIST

Sustainability in Business: Performing at High Levels Without Burning Out

- ☐ Identify self-care practices you're already doing and create your baseline plan.
- ☐ Circle the different self-care examples you most resonate with (making sure there's at least one for each of the six categories).
- ☐ Create your project self-care plan and share it with your coach, team, or colleagues.
- ☐ Integrate Gupta's 55:5 model and prioritize by scheduling it in your calendar.

ADDITIONAL RESOURCES TO SUPPORT YOU!

GET THE AUDIOBOOK + THE PROFESSIONAL COACHING BUSINESS TOOL KIT

Receive the free audiobook PLUS our Professional Coaching Business Tool Kit, a valuable download including the Professional Coach's Blueprint, the Clarity Quadrant, the budget template, and cash flow report template.

→ Download it at https://theprofessionalcoachbook.com/toolkit

ATTEND A FREE COACHING BUSINESS WORKSHOP

Ready to roll up your sleeves and start implementing? Attend our free online workshop webinar series to go deeper into the ideas in this book and put them into practice.

→ Sign up for free at https://theprofessionalcoachbook.com/workshop

JOIN US IN PERSON FOR OUR 3-DAY LIVE EVENT!

Discover how to implement the right success structures for your business to grow and thrive with ease in our 3-day intensive training event.

→ Reserve your spot at https://theprofessionalcoachbook.com/live

A REQUEST

Thank You for Reading My Book!

I would love hearing what you thought about the book. Please leave me a helpful review on Amazon!

Thanks so much,
— *Melinda Cohan*

GRATITUDES

It takes a village! I am profoundly grateful for those in my life who helped birth this book into existence, either directly or indirectly. A deep, heartfelt *thank you* to . . .

Danny Iny for sparking the idea of a second book, a desire I didn't even know I had until my hand shot up in the air and the words blurted out of my mouth: "I'll write that!

Michelle Falzon for teaching me your Create Without Burnout Cycle so my life could be even more amazing. And to Sebastian Night who took Michelle's cycle and applied it to the book-writing process. Thank you for that spark! I loved every part of the writing process as a result of following that cycle. I experienced a sense of flow and magic through the whole project

Victoria Labalme for modeling how to be impeccable in the book writing process that honors the reader's experience, and all involved. The details matter and I appreciate you teaching me just what that means when publishing a book.

Margaret Lynch Raniere for writing the foreword and adding in your magic to this message. I'm so grateful our paths crossed all those years ago in that mastermind.

Kate Steinbacher, my first coach and business partner. Wow! We created some epic adventures in our years of building and growing The Coaches Console together. I believe we mastered "taking care of hearts while taking care of business" and having a blast doing it. Thank you for opening me to a whole new world and a whole new life

My Coaches Console Core Team—Cosmin, Lori, Stephanie, Marjolein, and Amber. I couldn't do most of what I do without the support of each of you. Thank you for being the most magnificent team. Cos for being Director of Magic (and cooking all our meals when we're together), Lori for teaching us "no yucky work," Stephanie for always keeping us laughing and keeping us calm when things get crazy, Marjolein for your amazing ability to navigate all the details, and Amber for your grace and fun. It's more than business, it's family and I love each of you!

My coach team for being badass, deeply loving, extremely generous, and talented coaches who demonstrate impeccable professionalism and fierce fun simultaneously. Thank you for how you each show up in the world and let your light shine!

My students, for their courage to believe in themselves to take this journey in the first place and for allowing me the honor of being their guide. And a special shout-out to Ailish Pal. Your "Moment of Truth" post in our community summed up the reason that I get up every day and do this work. You wrote, "When I was faced with making the decision to invest in this program and in myself, a deep truth came up in me. It was like a big slap in the face. It was

GRATITUDES

the first time I realized that what had held me back from starting my business was that a part of me didn't believe I could do it. . . . I have done a lot of things in my life that others have viewed as courageous, but nothing has compared to taking this step to believe in and invest in myself at this level." Thank you for trusting me to be your guide and for believing in yourself! (Yes, she gave me her blessing to include her post here.)

Dave Cohan for being my warrior. I love us and how we create our lives together. It's the inspiration from our love that fuels the magic of all that I do and all that I am.

Mom for showing up in magical ways, at the most perfect moments to keep my inspiration flowing. Thank you from the other side of the veil and for celebrating with me in Spirit. Butterfly kisses to you.

Dad for infusing fun and spirit in me throughout my entire life. It's the deep love that we have as father-daughter that helps me believe in myself every day and have the courage to go after big dreams, like a second book. Thanks, Dad! And, yes, we are having fun!

Stephanie Burger, thank you for being the best sister and reminding me to not take life so seriously and to have outrageous fun in all that I do.

Dylan and Danielle. I am so proud of who you each are becoming. It is a sacred honor to be your stepmother and I'm grateful to be part of your lives.

Lindsay McKinnon and Nell Daniel, my Sister Goddesses and wing women extraordinaire. You were there to celebrate the writing milestones and held space for me as I expanded and evolved my way through this book writing adventure. Thank you for the countless brags, swamps, desires, and trinities that birth us into existence. I'm grateful for your witnessing of my journey and for the unconditional love you share.

Rob and Rhonda Moseley for the standing invitation to the fire pit in the evenings to mark the celebration part of my writing cycle after completing a chapter.

Julie Haase, Nora Bellot, and the entire team at The Writer's Ally for making the editing and publishing process flow so well. Thank you for helping bring the best out of this book.

And last, but not least... My gratitude for the Universe, Spirit, God, and Goddess for channeling and co-creating the message that wanted to come forth through this book. Thank you for always having my back and dazzling and delighting me every day!

REFERENCES

Introduction

LaRosa, John. "Top 6 Things to Know About the Personal Coaching Industry." MarketResearch.com. May 14, 2018. https://blog.marketresearch.com/top-6-things-to-know-about-the-personal-coaching-industry

Lumia. "The Ultimate Guide to Life Coach Salaries." October 15, 2023. https://www.lumiacoaching.com/blog/ultimate-guide-life-coach-salaries.

Morris, C. and S. Feldman. "The Pandemic Inspired 1 in 5 Americans to Reevaluate Their Lives." *Ipsos*. October 5, 2023. https://www.ipsos.com/en-us/news-polls/pandemic-inspired-1-5-americans-reevaluate-their-lives.

PricewaterhouseCoopers and International Coaching Federation. "2023 ICF Global Coaching Study Executive Summary." *International Coaching Federation*. Accessed November 2023, https://coachingfederation.org/research/global-coaching-study.

Sharpe, M., and A. Spencer. "Many Americans Say They Have Shifted Their Priorities Around Health and Social Activities During COVID-19." *Pew Research Center.* August 18, 2022. https://www.pewresearch.org/short-reads/2022/08/18/many-americans-say-they-have-shifted-their-priorities-around-health-and-social-activities-during-covid-19/.

Verified Market Research. "Online Coaching Platforms Market Size and Forecast." , accessed November 2023. https://www.verifiedmarketresearch.com/product/u-s-global-online-coaching-platforms-market/.

Zhou, Luisa. "The Coaching Industry Market Size in 2024." *Luisa Zhou.* Accessed November 2023. https://www.luisazhou.com/blog/coaching-industry-market-size/.

Navigating the Book

Falzon, Michelle. "Create Without Burnout." *Create Without Burnout.* November 2015. http://createwithoutburnout.com.

Thomashauer, Regena. *Pussy: A Reclamation.* Carlsbad, CA: Hay House LLC, 2016.

Villoldo, Alberto, Colette Baron-Reid, and Marcela Lobos. *Mystical Shaman Oracle Guidebook.* Carlsbad, CA: Hay House LLC, 2018.

REFERENCES

The Natural Evolution of a Coaching Business

"Amateur." *Google's English Dictionary as provided by Oxford Languages*. 1997. Accessed November 2023. https://languages.oup.com/google-dictionary-en/

"Amateur." *Online Etymology Dictionary*. September 18, 2022. https://www.etymonline.com/word/amateur.

de Wal, Aletta. "Hobbyist, Amateur, or Professional Artist - Which Are You?" *EmptyEasel.com*. January 2, 2011. https://emptyeasel.com/2011/02/01/hobbyist-amateur-or-professional-artist-which-are-you/.

Dixit, Vivek. "Being an Amateur Is Not a Bad Thing." *Medium*. March 4, 2021. https://vivekwrites.medium.com/being-an-amateur-is-not-a-bad-thing-ec573350b723 .

Hokuf, Jackson. "From Amateur to Professional: How to Become a Pro Golfer." *Curated*. May 28, 2023. https://www.curated.com/journal/155002/.

Indeed. "Hobby vs Business: Pros and Cons." *Indeed*. Accessed November 2023. https://www.indeed.com/hire/c/info/hobby-vs-business-pros-and-cons.

Internal Revenue Service. "Here's How to Tell the Difference Between a Hobby and a Business for Tax Purposes." *IRS Tax Tips*. April 13, 2022. https://www.irs.gov/newsroom/heres-how-to-tell-the-difference-between-a-hobby-and-a-business-for-tax-purposes.

Internal Revenue Service. "'Trade or Business' Defined." *IRS*. Accessed February 2024. https://www.irs.gov/charities-non-profits/trade-or-business-defined.

McIntyre, Charles-Edouard. "Hobby, Amateur, Professional - How You Treat Your Career Will Determine How It Treats You." *Medium*. May 19, 2023 from The Startup. https://medium.com/swlh/hobby-amateur-professional-1c475b9ed5c8.

Pressfield, Steven. *Turning Pro: Tap Your Inner Power and Create Your Life's Work*. New York: Black Irish Entertainment, 2012.

The Professional Coach's Journey to Success

The Chief Outsider. "7 Ways Not to Screw Up Your Value Proposition." *Chief Outsiders*. October 10, 2017. https://www.chiefoutsiders.com/blog/not-screw-up-value-proposition.

Fellows, Emily. "3 Common Mistakes in Value Proposition Creation." *Asgard*. January 12, 2023. https://www.asgardmarketing.co.uk/insights/3-common-mistakes-in-value-proposition-creation.

Laja, Peep. "Unique Value Proposition: How to Create a UVP (With 7 Examples)." *CXL*. December 16, 2023. https://cxl.com/blog/value-proposition-examples-how-to-create/.

REFERENCES

Pillar 1

Collins, Jim. *Good to Great: Why Some Companies Make the Leap . . . and Others Don't*. New York: Collins, 2001.

Norcross, J. C. and D. J. Vangarelli. "The Resolution Solution: Longitudinal Examination of New Year's Change Attempts." *Journal of Substance Abuse* 1(2) (1988–89):127–34. https://doi.org/10.1016/s0899-3289(88)80016-6.

Ruiz, don Miguel. *The Four Agreements: A Practical Guide to Personal Freedom (A Toltec Wisdom Book)*. San Rafael: Amber Allen, 1997.

WebMD Editorial Contributors. Bhandari, S. MD. "What Is Martyr Complex?" *WebMD*. February 25, 2024. https://www.webmd.com/mental-health/what-is-a-martyr-complex.

Pillar 2

Azulay, Yossi. "Entrepreneurs Make More Than 1,000 Decisions a Day! What's the Key for Successful Decisions?" *Medium*. March 27, 2019. Entrepreneurs Make More than 1,000 Decisions a Day! What's the Key for Successful Decisions?', *Medium* https://medium.com/@yossi.azulay/entrepreneurs-make-more-than-1-000-decisions-a-day-whats-the-key-for-successful-decisions-6d9a4e6c1beb.

Sauer, Jeff. "Are You Just Another Hard Worker . . . Or A Smart Worker?" *Data Driven*. August 19, 2022. https://datadrivenu.com/working-hard-vs-smart/.

Pillar 3

Port, Michael. *Book Yourself Solid: The Fastest, Easiest, and Most Reliable System for Getting More Clients Than You Can Handle Even If You Hate Marketing and Selling.* Hoboken: Wiley, 2006.

Pillar 4

Cohan, Melinda, host. "How to Wow Without Overwhelm with Jason Freidman." Mirasee FM. *Just Between Coaches.* September 27, 2023. Podcast, Mp3. https://mirasee.com/blog/podcasts/how-to-wow-without-overwhelm-jason-friedman/.

Cottrill Research, Author. "Various Survey Statistics: Workers Spend Too Much Time Searching for Information." *Cottrill Research.* https://cottrillresearch.com/various-survey-statistics-workers-spend-too-much-time-searching-for-information/.

Dloo. "Federated Search: The Importance of Being Able to Find Information." *Armedia.* October 30, 2013. https://armedia.com/blog/federated-search-the-importance-of-being-able-to-find-information/.

McLaren, Stu. 2016–2020. *The Membership Experience* [Course notes]. Searchie.io.

Wills, Brayn. "Does Your Workforce Spend Too Much Time Searching for Information?" *ProProfs Knowledge Base.* February 20, 2024. https://www.proprofskb.com/blog/workforce-spend-much-time-searching-information/.

REFERENCES

Pillar 5

Johnson, Whitney. "Celebrate to Win." *Harvard Business Review*. January 26, 2022. https://hbr.org/2022/01/celebrate-to-win.

McDade, Sean. "Customer Loss During Onboarding." *ABA Banking Journal*. August 15, 2016. https://bankingjournal.aba.com/2016/08/customer-loss-during-onboarding/.

Pillar 6

Grupa, Tom. "Cost to Hire Interior Designer or Decorator." *Home Guide of Liaison, Inc.* April 5, 2023. https://homeguide.com/costs/interior-designer-cost.

Stanny, Barbara. *Overcoming Underearning: A Five-Step Plan to a Richer Life.* New York: Collins, 2007.

Stanny, Barbara. *Sacred Success: A Course in Financial Miracles*. Dallas: BenBella Books, 2014.

Stanny, Barbara. *Secrets of Six-Figure Women: Surprising Strategies to Up Your Earnings and Change Your Life.* New York: Collins, 2002.

Thumbtack. "How Much Do Private Yoga Lessons Cost?" *Thumbtack*. February 15, 2021. https://www.thumbtack.com/p/yoga-prices.

Pillar 7

Chopra, Deepak. "The Conscious Lifestyle: Awareness Skills—Paying Attention." *Deepak Chopra.* May 31, 2013. https://www.deepakchopra.com/articles/the-conscious-lifestyle-awareness-skills-paying-attention/.

Cohan, Melinda, host. "Banishing Burnout with Michelle Falzon." Mirasee FM. *Just Between Coaches.* July 6, 2023. Podcast, Mp3. https://mirasee.com/blog/podcasts/banishing-burnout-michelle-falzon/.

Dacy, Craig. "4 Reasons We Avoid Budgets." *Dacy Financial Coaching.* March 3, 2022. https://craigdacy.com/2022/03/03/.

Ramsey, Dave. *The Total Money Makeover: A Proven Plan for Financial Fitness.* Thomas Nelson, 2003.

Wilson, Ann. *The Wealth Chef: Recipes to Make Your Money Work Hard, So You Don't Have To.* Carlsbad, CA: Hay House LLC, 2015.

Sustainability in Business

Butler, Lisa D., Kelly A. Mercer, Katie McClain-Meeder, and Dana Horne. "Six Domains of Self-Care: Attending to the Whole Person." *Journal of Human Behavior in the Social Environment.* January 2019. 29:1, 107-124, DOI: 10.1080/10911359.2018.1482483. https://www.researchgate.net/publication/330232181/.

REFERENCES

Gupta, Suneel. *Everyday Dharma: 8 Essential Practices for Finding Success and Joy in Everything You Do*. San Francisco: HarperOne, 2023.

Harvard Health Publishing. "Endorphins: The Brain's Natural Pain Reliever." *Harvard Medical School*. July 20, 2021. https://www.health.harvard.edu/mind-and-mood/endorphins-the-brains-natural-pain-reliever.

Perry, Elizabeth. "How to Release Endorphins and What They Are." *Better Up*. February 1, 2023. https://www.betterup.com/blog/how-to-release-endorphins.

Talbot-Kelly, Michael. "Self-Care & Neuroscience." *Michael Talbot-Kelly*. July 1, 2019. https://michaeltalbotkelly.com/self-care-neuroscience/.

Uda, Rachel. "Looking for More Joy in Your Job? 'Everyday Dharma' Shows Us the Path." *Katie Couric Media*. September 27, 2023. https://katiecouric.com/lifestyle/workplace/everyday-dharma-suneel-gupta/.

World Health Organization. "Burn-Out an 'Occupational Phenomenon': International Classification of Diseases." *World Health Organization*. May 28, 2019. https://www.who.int/news/item/28-05-2019-burn-out-an-occupational-phenomenon-international-classification-of-diseases.

Conclusion

Williamson, Marianne. *A Return to Love: Reflections on the Principles* of A Course in Miracles. New York: Collins, 1993.

ABOUT THE AUTHOR

Melinda Cohan achieved fast success when she launched her first coaching business, quickly replacing the income from her previous job as a workplace-efficiency interior designer.

In 2004, she started coaching other coaches to grow their businesses, based on a vision she'd scribbled on the back of a napkin to "eliminate the burdens and distractions of coaches" using her expertise in designing systems and processes. She became the cofounder and CEO of The Coaches Console, now a seven-figure software, training, and coaching company that has helped more than one hundred thousand coaches create profitable and thriving businesses.

Cohan's work has given her an insider's view of the coaching industry: every kind of coach, every kind of business model, every kind of challenge and solution, and every shift in the coaching industry. In her first book, *The Confident Coach*, she shares her insights so you can take the complexity out of your coaching business and turn your passion and talent into profits. Cohan also hosts *Just Between Coaches*, a podcast focusing on the challenges coaches face and how to overcome them. She recently celebrated its 130th episode.

THE PROFESSIONAL COACH

When she isn't coaching, Cohan and her husband, Dave, enjoy the outdoors (especially skiing). They love organizing and leading travel adventure trips around the world for their local ski and adventure club. They also enjoy going to concerts, music festivals, and football games, and creating adventures with their family.